Steps
to the
Future

Steps

to the

Future

What we need to know before
we can think strategically
about the church's future in Britain

Peter Brierley

All royalties from this book will go towards the cost of
further research for the church

Christian Research and Scripture Union

2000

First British edition 2000

ISBNs

Scripture Union:	1 85999 446 6
Christian Research:	1 85321 136 2

Published jointly by Christian Research and Scripture Union

Christian Research, Vision Building, 4 Footscray Road, Eltham, London SE9 2TZ

Tel: 020 8294 1989 Fax: 020 8294 0014

Email: admin@christian-research.org.uk

Website: www.christian-research.org.uk

Scripture Union, 207–209 Queensway, Bletchley, Milton Keynes, Bucks MK2 2EB

Tel: 01908 856000 Fax: 01908 856111

Email: info@scriptureunion.org.uk

Website: www.scripture.org.uk

British Library Cataloguing Data
A catalogue record for this book is available from the British Library.

Printed and bound by Creative Print and Design (Wales) Ebbw Vale

Contents

Foreword

Tremendous challenges face the Christian church as the third millennium dawns. How can the Gospel of Jesus Christ be effectively demonstrated in all its relevance, reality and power? What can we do to accommodate to changing cultural pressures and to shifting population profiles? Specifically - and these are two key areas with which Scripture Union is ultimately concerned - how can we arrest the decline in personal Bible reading, and what can we do to invigorate the nurturing of children and young people within our churches?

These are huge questions. Fortunately, we have a loving God whose own heart also desires to see communities of believers transformed and renewed by his living Word.

Yet how does the local church begin to form a viable strategy for change and growth that will see its kingdom vision fulfilled in the community?

Being informed is a good start and *Steps to the Future* provides Christians with a wealth of research data. It could so easily have been a depressing read! Yet this book is much more than a report highlighting the struggles and challenges within the Christian world. Peter Brierley, whose name has been synonymous for many years with excellent in-depth research for the Christian church, gives us valuable insights and suggestions for positive and practical forward moves.

Minister, lay leader, concerned believer – I encourage you to read through this book prayerfully, sharing it with your church. Aim not simply to absorb information, but look to be equipped to respond to the needs and demands of our age.

A final point! Jesus had little to say to religious people with closed minds, but his power was instantly available to the desperate. Renewal comes to churches who are desperate to experience God's power.

"Blessed are those who know their need of God: the Kingdom of Heaven is theirs."

Peter Kimber
Chief Executive, *Scripture Union*

Introduction

In 1998 a major Christian agency approached Christian Research and asked us to undertake an assignment. Before doing so, Christian Research felt it necessary to think through some of the factors affecting church life in the UK today.

Some of these factors were demographic, some were social, some were cultural and some religious. We found it useful to group these factors and then work through how important they might be for the organisation concerned.

Obviously that part of the process is confidential. The factors themselves, however, are not, and we felt that they could be useful for others thinking towards the future.

That is how this book came to be written. Apart from taking out references to the organisation concerned, the actual text of that initial report has only been altered for editorial reasons. It can therefore be used by clergy and church leaders, by Christian leaders or lay people in other contexts, to see a wide range of issues facing the church. In some places, some of the facts make uncomfortable reading. Because of the nature of the research material and the associated analyses, some of the chapters may seem so full of information that you need to allow time to reflect.

We would suggest the following way of handling this book:

1) Read or look through the book in some detail first so you are familiar with its contents and general direction.

2) Then go through each chapter and list the issues identified. In some chapters this will be quite a long list. There will be some overlap between one chapter and the next.

3) You may find it helpful to group the items on your list in some way. These were the categories we used:
· Church trends
· Evangelism trends
· Leadership trends
· Society trends
· Sunday School trends
· Young people trends.
(We ended up with 162 items across these 6 groups!)

4) Evaluate each item on your list in relation to your own situation (church, organisation, etc) as being of high, medium or low importance.

5) Now take the items you have identified as of high importance and rate each on a scale from 1 (just important) to 10 (extremely important).

6) List the ones you have scored highest with the most important on top. You may wish to revise the marks you've given different factors. That's fine!

7) Now look at the top 3 or 5 or 7 of these – whatever constitutes a convenient break-point. What are the implications of these for your church or organisation?

8) Finally, the most crucial part of all: in the light of these considerations, decide what steps you are going to take in the next month to change these aspects of your church's or organisation's situation. Unless you are prepared to work through this step, it's not worth starting out down this path! This question will need to be prayed through also.

Happy reading, listing, thinking and praying! And may the Lord bless you and guide you as you consider what actions are most suitable.

Peter Brierley
Executive Director, *Christian Research*
March 2000

The European Context

Following the break-up of the USSR, the United Nations redefined the world's continents in 1992. Prior to this date, the USSR had been allocated in its entirety to Europe; now only the six most western countries are defined as being in Europe, while the rest are deemed to be in Asia. Asia is by far the most populous continent: in 1995, it had 60% of the world's 5,740 million people; Africa and Europe came next with 13% each, leaving the two Americas and Oceania (Australia, New Zealand, Pacific territories) to make up the rest.

However, the Asian Christian church is the smallest in any continent. Of the world's 1,614 million Christians in 1995, Asians were just 16% of the total. Europe has the highest number (27%), with the two Americas between them accounting for 41%, leaving 15% for Africa and 1% for Oceania. Figure 1 shows these relative proportions.

These 1,614 million Christians are 28% of the world population. In addition, 18% are Muslim, and 13% Hindu.[1]

Figure 1: World and Christian population (millions) by continent, 1995

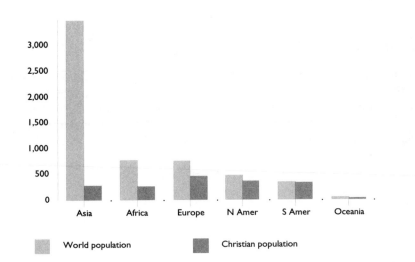

Europe within the world context

The Christian community throughout the world grew threefold in the first 90 years of the twentieth century. Table 1 shows that in 1900 over two-thirds (71%) of the world's Christians lived in Europe; sixty years later, this had dropped to under half (46%), and by 1990 to less than a third (30%). However, set against this decline has been dramatic growth in Asia and Africa particularly, where proportions have doubled, trebled (and more!) during the same period. The upper three continents in Table 1 form the Western world, and the bottom three the so-called Third World.

Table 1: World Christian community, 1900, 1960 and 1990

	Percentage of total community		
	1900 %	1960 %	1990 %
Europe	71	46	30
North America	11	23	21
Oceania[1]	1	1	1
Africa	2	7	15
Asia	4	7	14
South America	11	16	19
TOTAL in millions (=100%)	554	924	1,512

[1] Mainly Australia and New Zealand

Institutional Christianity

An 'institutional church' is defined as one which is, in at least one country of the world, the state church. On that basis, the Roman Catholics, Presbyterians, Orthodox, Lutherans and Anglicans qualify. Table 2 shows the percentage of Christendom in each continent which was part of one of these; figures for 1900 are unfortunately not readily available.

Table 2: Institutional world Christian community, 1960 and 1990

	Percentage in institutional denominations	
	1960 %	1990 %
Europe	98	97
North America	67	68
Oceania	80	80
Africa	76	63
Asia	80	55
South America	97	86
OVERALL	**88**	**78**

The denominations deemed to be 'non-institutional' are the Baptists, Indigenous Churches (mostly in Africa), Methodists, Pentecostals and the many other smaller, but worldwide denominations (such as the Salvation Army, Christian Brethren, Quakers, Mennonites, etc).

Table 2 shows that not only does Europe have the highest percentage of Christians in institutional churches, but that that percentage hardly changed between 1960 and 1990, despite the growth of the Pentecostal, New and other charismatic churches in the UK and elsewhere. On the other hand, institutionalism has decreased in the Third World. This is because of the huge and rapid growth worldwide of the smaller denominations, including Pentecostalism; this last increased from 1% of Christendom in 1960 to 6% in 1990, and is forecast to grow to 8% by 2010.

Figure 2: Percentage of Christians in institutional churches, 1960 and 1990

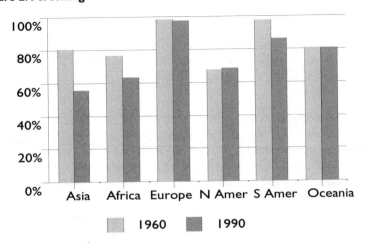

The continents in which institutionalism has decreased most are the ones which have experienced the most rapid growth in the Christian church. This suggests that institutionalism is less advantageous to the church than it used to be – if it ever was. (Not everyone would agree that Constantine took the right action in AD 313!)

In Europe, however, institutionalism is still dominant, and in our Christian witness it forms the culture within which we have to operate. Some of its characteristics are:

- large numbers of nominal Christians
- danger of complacency based on position, numbers and tradition
- reactionary attitude to rapid change
- inflexible structures
- unwillingness to experiment

It is easy to observe all these in Europe, and especially the UK, today. Perhaps the first, and the second which derives from it, are the more important factors in shaping attitudes.

In his introductory chapter to *British Social Trends 1900-2000*[2], Professor Halsey says that twentieth-century institutions provided five systems for society as a whole:

- production (manufacturing)
- reproduction
- power and authority
- ritual
- communication

All these are in place in the UK today. This book intends to examine the fourth of these – the system of ritual.

Nominalism

The Oxford English Dictionary defines nominalism as 'existing in name only, not real or actual'. The implication is that 'nominal Christians' are not real or actual Christians. There are two consequences of such a conclusion:

- **We are describing a static mode.** But if nominal Christians are moving towards becoming real or actual Christians, this description is incorrect. If nominal Christians are those who have left behind an intensity, an involvement, an interest, and are *moving away from something*, then they are not static. If, however, nominal Christians are those who have accepted an inadequate or misrepresented form of belief, and have no opportunity to *move towards something*, they are truly static. What became clearer in the 1990s through various pieces of research is that nominalism is often less of a 'state' (that is, a permanent position) than a time of transition (that is, a position which applies for a period, sometimes many years).

- **The relationship between belief and behaviour is not apparent.** The dictionary definition probably tends more towards belief than behaviour, but Christian nominalism seems more related to behaviour than belief, even if only defined negatively ('not a regular attender'). What nominal Christians might or might not believe is only one part of the equation.

Jesus' parable of the sower (or, more accurately, the soils) defines different groups according to behaviour, not faith. He describes three 'states': people are either inside the kingdom, outside it, or somewhere in between. The last group tends to gravitate towards those outside, because they can't stand the pressure ('tribulation or persecution … on account of the word'[3]), or because they prefer the alternatives ('cares of the world … delight in riches … desire for other things'[4]). In both these scenarios, other priorities prevailed. We are seeing exactly the same patterns of behaviour with regular churchgoers today. Are they becoming more nominal as a consequence?

Theologians disagree as to whether the parable of the sower is 'prescriptive' (saying what *will* happen when the gospel is proclaimed) or 'descriptive' (saying what is observed to happen). In either case, the four types of soil are not given any kind of quantitative assessment, so we cannot assume that the four states are equal, or that one group is larger than another. The descriptive model suggests that the four modes are stationary; the prescriptive model could suggest that there might be a transition between one type and another.

In 1991 Peter Cotterell, then president of the British Church Growth Association, said that the European church had six problems, of which the first was nominalism. 'Calling people nominal Christians when they never go to church simply confuses the issue of evangelism,' he explained in one of his presidential addresses.

Perhaps the word 'nominal' is too pejorative. We are not out to alienate nominal Christians but to bring about change, and to win them to a deeper, more relevant, faith. These comments will be interpreted by some as suggesting that change is essential to progress. This certainly would appear to be the case if the church is to rediscover the Christianity of the New Testament.

Nominalism is a key issue of the day, and not just in institutional Europe. One of the papers given at the International Lausanne Consultation on Nominalism held in the UK in December 1998[5] listed twelve different types of 'nominality'[6] (described in Chapter 2). Even if nominal Christians could be accurately quantified in 1990 (as Table 1 might suggest), it is even less certain that they can be so a decade later.

How many churches?

Table 3 highlights the differences between the institutional Christianity of the Western world and the expansionist Christianity in the Third World during the latter part of the twentieth century.

Table 3: Numbers of churches worldwide, 1960 and 1990

| | Churches/Congregations | | | | | |
| | Number in thousands | | Per 10,000 pop | | Members per church | |
	1960	1990	1960	1990	1960	1990
Europe	302	325	4.6	4.1	811	786
North America	346	493	12.8	11.6	393	402
Oceania	21	38	13.3	14.1	215	219
Africa	126	476	4.5	7.4	272	228
Asia	104	529	0.6	1.7	322	200
South America	35	220	2.4	7.5	2,656	806
TOTAL/OVERALL	**934**	**2,081**	**3.1**	**3.9**	**585**	**410**

The actual number of churches increased by 28% between 1960 and 1990 in the Western world, but by 362% in the Third World. As a consequence, their number per 10,000 population almost doubled in Africa, and trebled in Asia and South America. Pentecostalism has replaced some Roman Catholicism in Latin America, seen in Table 3 by the huge number of established churches started in South America, the large majority of which are Pentecostal, and the subsequent large fall in numbers per church – a change which David Martin[7], formerly Professor of Sociology at the London School of Economics, observes with great perceptiveness. Why the huge growth in Latin American Pentecostalism? Partly because of its link with social action, and perhaps because of the increase in education and literacy.

Figure 3: Churches per 10,000 population, 1960 and 1990

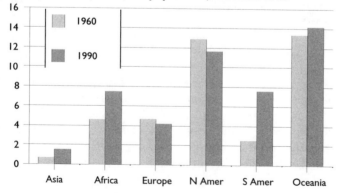

In the UK in 1960 we had 10.7 churches per 10,000 population, a figure which fell to 8.6 by 1990. During those thirty years, the population increased but the number of new churches being started was unable to compensate for the massive number of closures in the large denominations, particularly the Methodists, Church of Scotland and Church of England. Even so, in 1990 the UK had 15% of Europe's churches, with twice as many per 10,000 population as in Europe as a whole. They are, however, only a fifth (1960) or a sixth (1990) the size of a European church, reflecting the Protestant heritage of the UK, and the relatively small proportions of Catholics, Lutherans and Orthodox Christians, all of which have larger churches.

Table 3 shows that South American churches are the largest in the world; this is due to their large numbers of Catholic churches, which tend to be very big. The same is true in the UK. In 1990, the Catholics had a Mass attendance in the UK averaging 507 people per church, the Presbyterians a membership of 221, Anglicans 105, and all others 74.[8]

Other factors of European life

Peter Cotterell also drew attention to another factor in 1991 which is still important today. He mentioned the infiltration of materialism in many churches, referring to the 'Prosperity Gospel' some were proclaiming, and the lack of appropriate training in many colleges. Certainly London Bible College, of which he was then principal, as well as other colleges like All Nations and the International Christian College, have introduced many new courses over the last few years, and now teach sociology, pastoral theology, counselling, research and related topics.

Other facets, however, remain the same or have grown worse:

- the fragmentation of the church: often means the combined strength of the church is not apparent
- pluralism: all religions are seen as equal, and the uniqueness of Christianity is held by fewer people, even committed Christians[9]
- the occult: there are now 7,000 committed Satanists in Germany, according to a recent report,[10] and their number and overt activities are growing

Professor Bill Wagner, in his doctoral thesis on European churches, identified three problems of European Free churches:[11]

- lack of identity
- minority complex
- lack of resources

While these are undoubtedly true of many groups in mainland Europe, they are less true in the UK where many smaller churches, for example, are welcomed into local evangelical fellowships or joint church councils. Their resource stringency is true, however – and that doesn't just apply to the Free churches!

So what does all this mean?

Summarising, these thoughts indicate that:

- European Christianity is much less important worldwide at the end of the twentieth century than at the beginning. At that time, it set the model for the rest of the world; today, while still important, we need to learn from our Asian and African brothers and sisters.
- European Christianity is dominated by institutionalism and the deadening impact of the bureaucracy that this brings. Our major denominations need to recover their freedom in Christ by encouraging less rather than more central control. Cicero wrote, 'The last act of an institution is to write the rules for its own behaviour.' We are in danger of doing just that.
- Christianity in Europe and in the UK is riddled with nominalism. We have not only the situation where people are 'believing without belonging',[12] but also those who are 'belonging without believing'. Both positions pose theological and pastoral problems. We cannot stand on the sidelines of nominality.
- The church in Europe and in the UK urgently needs to reappraise what makes churches grow in these contexts. We need examples of success, and the ability to identify the reasons for that success. Perhaps publishing books modelling such churches, such as MARC Europe's *Ten Growing Churches* (1984), would help.
- Many nominal Christians are 'ex-churched' rather than un-churched. While part of the task of churches therefore is reaching people, the essence of the gospel, the other part is keeping people, the essence of discipleship.
- We need to recover our confidence in the gospel, perhaps best done by renewing our vision of what it is we believe God wants us to become over the next five or ten years – individually as leaders, bodily as churches, and corporately as denominations.

Church People in the UK

In August 1998, the *Guardian* commended[1] the opening of the new 4,000-seater auditorium (double the capacity of either Westminster Abbey or St Paul's Cathedral) by Kingsway International Christian Centre in Hackney, east London. The article contained details of the church's stage – which has room for a 300-strong choir, a ten-piece band and grand piano – and the three giant TV monitors which magnify events for those at the back, and also transmit them, via satellite, to 70 million homes in Europe and Africa. The Senior Minister, the Rev Matthew Ashimolowo, comes from Nigeria, and started the church in 1992.

'The Church is bleeding to death, says Carey' ran the *Daily Telegraph* headline just four months later, reporting the Archbishop of Canterbury, Dr George Carey's speech at the World Council of Churches' assembly in Zimbabwe.[2] He said that the church was facing a crisis – a moment of decision which could end in either opportunity or judgement – which, if it did not 'lead us to Christ, will surely end in decline for our churches today'.

As if to subscribe to Dr George Carey's prognosis, to profess faith could be to court disapproval. For example, in the United States, Yale law professor Stephen Carter noted that 'one is allowed to have any view on abortion so long as it derives from ethical or practical or socio-logical or medical considerations. But should someone ... oppose abortion for reasons of faith, he is accused of trying to impose his religious beliefs on others.' G K Chesterton's statement that tolerance is the virtue of people who do not believe in anything needs amplifying. Tolerance has also become the virtue of people who profess to believe something; it is regarded as the hallmark of 'mature belief'.[3]

How then do we look at those involved with the church in the UK? There are many characteristics of church life in the UK which have relevance for the work of both churches and para-church agencies, and it is simplest to start by a general description or model.

The basic framework

There are three broad measures for describing Christian people, at least in the Western nations.

Community

The Christian community has been defined as 'All those who would positively identify with belonging to a church even if they may only attend irregularly, or were just baptised as a child'.[4] Another definition is, 'Those who belong to a particular denomination, however loosely. If Anglican, Roman Catholic, Lutheran, Orthodox or Presbyterian, they will usually approximate to the number baptised in that country'.[5] The Methodists keep a 'Community Roll' for each church.

In the Northern Ireland population census, which includes a question on religion, the Christian community is simply taken as the total number who tick a box indicating their 'religious allegiance'[6] or preference. Some equate the Christian community to Christian 'adherents'.[7] The broad thrust of these definitions is clear: all those in a particular country who would call themselves Christian.

In Britain, people going into hospital or prison are asked their religion. Many people simply reply 'C of E' (Church of England), or 'Methodist' or 'RC' (Roman Catholic), even if they have no current connection with that particular church. The community figure seeks to represent the totality of all such people. In *Religious Trends No.1 1998/99*,[8] the figure is given as 65% of the entire population in 1995, a decrease from 72% in 1975. Similar percentages are available for every country in the world in the *World Churches Handbook*.[9]

Your religious community is normally considered the one into which you were born or baptised; in other words, you had no choice in the matter. It is interesting that in France some twenty Catholics, as a protest about the Pope's visit to their country because they no longer agree with the family planning and pro-life values he espouses, sought to be 'de-baptised' by French bishops in June and July 1996.[10] When doing some research in Scotland, we asked if people had ever regretted their infant baptism. All respondents said no, except one person who wished she hadn't after having been baptised as an adult.

Membership

Most denominations of the church unfortunately define membership differently! Thus in a Baptist church, membership is usually limited to those baptised as adults, whereas in an Anglican church members are often taken as those on the Electoral Roll (not to be confused with the local authority electoral roll). In some Pentecostal churches, membership is confined to those who are baptised, born again, speak in tongues and give evidence of living an active Christian life over at least six months.

The Roman Catholics, however, define their members as the 'baptised', which is equated above to church community. In Nigeria, if you wish to join the New Life Church, you have to give a positive answer to the question, 'When did you last pray for a miracle?' The variety of meaning extends to the ages of those counted as members: for Anglicans it comprises those aged sixteen and over, for Baptists fourteen and over, etc.

The value of membership figures is that they are frequently available for many decades, and even occasionally for centuries.[11] They have usually been collected using the same definition *within a particular denomination* and therefore the trends in the figures may be judged as accurate in that defined context.

It has been suggested that denominations which have the strictest membership criteria are likely to be those which grow fastest. There was some truth in this amongst the black Pentecostal denominations in the UK in the 1980s when the New Testament Church of God and the Church of Cherubim and Seraphim, for example, recorded attendance five times as great as their membership.[12] This has been confirmed by two studies in America, one in the 1970s amongst Conservative churches, and the other in the 1990s amongst Lutheran churches. 'Churches that reflect solid quality and quantity growth are those that are clear to declare specific tenets of belief'.[13]

It should be noted that membership and attendance are neither the same nor necessarily linked! The Baptist Union of Scotland had a special outreach programme in the mid-1980s. In their report they said, 'During 1985 there was a marked increase in church membership (7.8 persons per church against 4.8 in 1982) and a total of 1,149 first commitments. It was disturbing to note that of these only 50% were recorded as being baptised, and only 33% as joining the church.'[14]

Church membership in the UK has been decreasing: in 1975 it was 19% of the population, but by 1995 had dropped to 14%.[15]

Attendance

Church attendance is much easier to quantify – either people are there on a Sunday or they're not! Counting people present on a particular day therefore gives a uniformity to the numbers across all denominations. Attendance figures, however, are not always or universally collected, and even when regularly counted, will often be counted on different Sundays by different denominations.

There have been a number of church censuses which have counted people across every denomination on the same day. Two of these, the English Church Census of 1989[16] and the Scottish Church Census of 1994[17] give 10% and 14% respectively of the adult population (ie, aged fifteen and over) as attending church. Both counts excluded those who attended twice on a Sunday. These figures compare with 25% in Australia[18] and 42% in the United States.[19]

However, even here the accuracy may be questioned. Do the figures measure the number of attenders or the number of attendances? The numbers are not the same! In the case of the British church censuses, the number counted is the number of attenders, but these surveys still did not give any indication of the frequency with which each person actually attends - the 1998 *English Church Attendance Survey* did that.

Putting it together

Figure 4: Community, membership, attendance (not to scale)

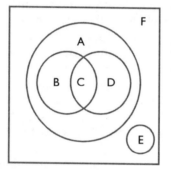

A = those who call themselves Christian but are not members or frequent attenders of any church: they may go at Christmas or Easter

B = regular church attenders but not members

C = regular attenders and members of their church

D = members but not regular attenders

E = members of another faith community

F = non-religious population

Alternative method of identification

There is an alternative way of exploring the above categories. When asked, 'Do you believe in God?' (defined in the Trinitarian manner!), 71% of British people answered yes,[20] providing an alternative definition of the Christian community.

The many sample surveys which have asked this question record positive replies in the 60–75% range. One of the best known is the annual *British Social Attitudes Survey*,[21] which has consistently asked the question, 'Do you regard yourself as belonging to any particular religion?' In 1983, 31% said they had no religion, and 2% a non-Christian religion, respectively 34% and 2% in 1989, supporting the figures given above.

The second question would be, 'Do you attend church regularly?' and the positive response would have been about 10% in Great Britain in 1990.[22] It is true that this question does not ask how regularly people attend, but we shall leave this aspect for the moment.

The third question would be, 'Are you a church member?' These answers would be the same as given above. These three sets of answers may be put together in the following chart:[23]

Figure 5: Religious structure of the population of Great Britain, 2000 and 1980

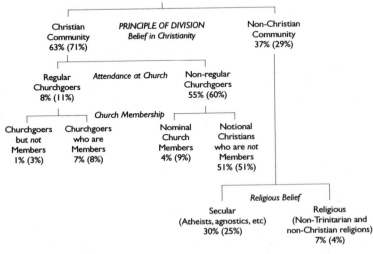

Figures in brackets give 1980 percentages

This chart indicates some specific categories:

- **nominal church members:** members of a church who do not regularly attend
- **notional Christians:** neither members nor regular attenders of a church, but who would say they were Christian
- regular churchgoers but not members who could be called **new Christians**
- regular church attenders who belong to their local church who could be called **'normal' Christians**
- **non-Christians:** members of non-Trinitarian churches, non-Christian religions and secular people (atheists, agnostics etc.)

This categorisation splits what others have called 'nominal' Christians into two groups – nominal and notional, the difference being that the former still retain their church membership. The difference is useful because the belief systems of nominal and notional Christians seem to be different.

Why so many nominal/notional Christians?

Figure 5 gives a Christian community in Great Britain in 2000 of 63% against a membership of 11% and attendance of 8%. The gap between the first two figures – 52% – *is the largest in the world!* Why do we have more notional Christians in this country than anywhere else? The then LSE sociologist, David Lyon (now Sociology Professor at Ottawa University), gave the following reasons:[24]

- This was no longer an age of faith as it was in Victorian times.
- The sense of the uniqueness of Christianity had been muted.
- There was a loss of intellectual confidence, essentially stemming from Darwin, but seen socially and culturally as well as intellectually.
- Many people had lost their religion and saw the world as losing theirs. He had in mind sociologist Max Weber, who lived in a world of rationalisation, intellectualisation and disenchantment, and assumed that everyone else did too.
- Christianity had become marginal in the lives many people led.
- Christianity had become a private, middle-class occupation. In her doctoral thesis, Melanie Cottrell said, 'Identity for middle-class people is divorced from the social structure, and people are forced in on themselves.'
- The 'Pendulum Church' swings from bureaucracy to 'destructured spontaneity', meaning that everyone does 'their own thing'.

Movement (1)

Figure 5 shows the changes between 1980 and 2000. They focus on three main areas:

- The decline in new Christians: fewer were being attracted into the churches in 2000 than in 1980. Each percentage point represents half a million people, so this 2% drop represents one million fewer people.
- In addition, another half a million churchgoing members were also lost in the period. Even the more committed have stopped going to church.
- The growth in the number of 'other religions': up from 4% to 7%, an increase again of about one and a half million people.

There was a decline in the number of nominal Christians – quite literally dying out – and no change in the number of notional Christians.

Movement (2)

There is, however, a kind of progression in these trends which cannot be illustrated with firm figures, but is shown with arrows in Figure 6.

- New Christians are those who start attending the church, coming from either a notional or non-Christian background.
- Many of these will eventually become church members.
- Some of these, especially perhaps when older, ill or lacking transport, move into the nominal category.
- Some of these eventually drop their church membership and become notional Christians.
- A very few notional Christians drop all pretence of Christianity.

Figure 6: Movement in the religious structure

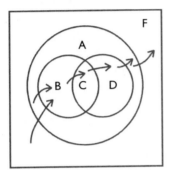

See key on page 12

The logical sequence in the above was perhaps valid for the experience of churchgoing and Christianity in Britain in the 1980s. It is, however, rightly called the 'old' model, because it no longer gives the full picture in the 1990s.

Movement (3)

In the 1990s, additional types of movement have developed, without necessarily invalidating the earlier movements. These are as follows, using the notation in Figure 7 below:

a)Some people have started going to church, but then stopped going. They may come back later. There is no question of progressing on to membership; that is not what they want. For example, some women now living on an estate near Dartford, Kent, had attended a church before they got married, but their husbands did not wish them to go to church, leaving them to look after the children. So the local vicar started a service on a Wednesday morning, which these ladies gladly attend while their husbands are at work and their children at school.

b)Others have started going to a church, say Church M. Then after a while they decide to try Church N, and maybe Churches P, Q and R as well. They may or may not return to Church M. These are people deliberately moving from one church to another. This often happens when church people move house to another part of the country, even though, for some, not very far from their previous home.

c)There are church members who leave their church for some reason, often because they move house, but who do not take up membership of the next church they start attending. This may be because it is, say, a Baptist church and they are Anglican, or it may be because they no longer wish to have the responsibilities of membership. This attitude can easily be encouraged when churches are unable to give good reasons why people should join them. To be able to vote for the churchwardens in the Church of England or at the AGM is hardly the most compelling reason!

d) Then there are church members who decide to try another church, perhaps only temporarily, or perhaps for longer. They may take out membership in their 'new' church without cancelling their old. We know several families who have switched churches, sometimes for positive reasons (their children enjoy the activities of Church X more than Church Y), and sometimes for negative reasons (can't stand the minister in Church Z).

e) There are also church members who drop out of the church scene for some considerable time. They just stop going to church, maybe to have more time for the family, maybe with the intention of returning sometime when the family has left home.

f) There is yet another group who have stopped attending church, and become essentially nominal in the above sense of the word, but who start attending church again, maybe when they've retired and got more time, or because their spouse dies and they want friendship, or to accompany their grandchildren, or for other reasons. There are a growing number in this group.

We thus have a new model, rather more complex than before, which can be illustrated as shown below:

Figure 7: Movement in the religious structure in the 1990s

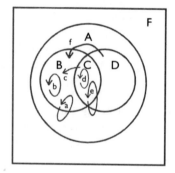

See key on page 12

Features of the religious structure at the beginning of the 21st century are:

- The religious community is static in numbers (forty-two million 1975 to 2000), but declining as a percentage of the increasing population.
- The Christian proportion of this group is declining because of the growth of other religions.
- Church membership is declining (21% between 1980 and 2000), partly because membership of most organisations in society generally is declining.[25] Three denominations are growing - the Orthodox, Pentecostal and New Churches - partly because they all started new congregations.
- Sunday attendance is also declining, partly because there is a decline in the frequency of attendance.
- There is a further movement implicit in Figure 7. How does the committed core group reach the outside non-committed group? By going through the notional group? There are some who say we should. But I would argue that we need distinctively different strategies for reaching the 30 million notional Christians in our land, the 18 million non-Christians and non-religious, the 4 million religious in other religions who are non-Christian, and maybe a different one again for the 2 million nominal church members who no longer attend. That's all assuming that the 5 million attenders are up to the job!

This last is a particular worry. A church leader in North Wales told a meeting of Operation Mobilisation leaders in their Quinta headquarters early in 1998, 'The churches of North Wales are not strong enough to take on the spiritual challenge of taking their land for Jesus and dealing with the spiritual and human opposition they encounter.'[26] This was in the light of the many empty churches or very small and elderly congregations in North Wales, reinforced by some hostility between the English and the Welsh communities in North Wales.

Frequency of church attendance

The question 'Do you go to church?' no longer has the connotation it once had. The implication behind an affirmative answer was that the respondent went every week. Not so now! At a 1993 Christmas carol service I sat behind someone I hadn't seen before, and asked if it was their first visit. 'Oh, no, we come regularly to this church,' they said. 'Every Christmas!' Between the 'twicers' who attend twice on Sunday (12% of churchgoers[27]), and the 'Christmas-specials' lies a whole range of attendance patterns.

In the week (first week of February 1997) that the Church of England announced a 3% drop in the number attending services, the largest for twenty years, an article appeared in the *Church Times* by the Rector of

West Monkton in the Diocese of Bath and Wells[28]. He said that when he first went to his church there were 150 people associated with it (the community). These divided into three groups of fifty: the first attended every week, the second came once a month, and the third came only at Easter and Christmas.

Ignoring the last group, the average weekly attendance was therefore 50 + 25% of 50 = 62 people. Now, twenty years later, the first group has decreased to forty people, largely through death, the second group has expanded to sixty, and the third group is much the same as it was. The weekly attendance is therefore now 40 + 25% of 60 = 55, a decline of 10%, but with the number associated with the church unchanged.

What measurements of it exist? The *British Social Attitudes* (BSA) Survey collects this information.[29] In 1997, the most recent year for which it was published, it found that 12% of the population claimed to attend weekly, 2% fortnightly, 6% monthly, 12% every six months, 5% once a year, 4% less than once a year, 24% never but were nevertheless 'religious', and 35% never went because they weren't 'religious'. Figures from the 1990 *European Values Study*[30] found 13% of the population attended weekly, 10% monthly, 12% at Christmas and Easter, 8% once a year, and 57% never (not distinguishing the last two groups of the BSA study).

These two sets of figures from entirely different sources are very close. The BSA figures indicate that on an average week, 12% attend + 1% of the fortnightly ones (half of 2%) + 1.5% of the monthly (quarter of 6%) + 0.5% of the six-monthlies (one 26th of 12%) + 0.1% of the annual (one 52nd of 5%), which comes to 15% to the nearest whole percentage, forgetting those who come less than once a year.

We can say, therefore, that 15% of the population might be expected in church every week, even though only 12% go every week. On the *European Values Study* data, the total figure would be 16%. In Australia, where the *National Church Life Survey*[31] put 11% of the population in church on an average Sunday, perhaps a further 2% would attend less than frequently[32], a total of 13%. These figures suggest a 'fringe' of about 20% of the population attending weekly, and acts as a kind of estimate into which to earth this look at nominalism. The 1998 *English Church Attendance Survey* updates these figures.[33]

Britain: a Christian country?

Many still say that 'Britain is a Christian country'. What does this mean when so few attend church on Sunday? Is church attendance the barometer? Clearly not. One cartoonist showed a greengrocer talking to the vicar, and saying to him, '… but I haven't seen you in my shop much recently, either'. In the autumn of 1995, the motor industry ran a series of advertisements with an implicit religious motif, and so did Littlewoods Pools. Neither would have done so if that motif was not recognisable by the majority of the population.

When the Pope visited Australia in November 1996, he spoke specifically about reaching those who had heard the gospel but who 'no longer
respond'. 'I am thinking,' he said, 'of those baptised in the faith who are
no longer actively present in the church. They are of many different types,
and the reasons for their absence from the community of Christ's faithful
are also many.'[34]

Is there any other evidence which would substantiate the broad 63%
Christian figure for Britain? Yes, there is:

- 49% of the babies born in 1996 were baptised as infants in a church.
- 44% of all weddings in 1996 were held in a church, and while this
  percentage will undoubtedly decrease further as more 'approved
  premises' other than registry offices are appointed, it does not necessarily follow that the percentage getting married for the first time
  choosing a church ceremony (60% in 1996) will necessarily decline so
  much or so fast. However, it should be noted that in 1997, 61% of
  Church of England parishes had fewer than ten marriages to conduct
  during the entire year.[35]
- Possibly as many as 90% of funerals in this country conclude with a
  religious ceremony.
- In 1990 some 71% of people said they believed in God,[36] although
  again this percentage is declining (76% in 1981). Belief that God is a
  Spirit has remained unchanged since the 1940s; belief that God is a
  Person has dropped from 43% to 31% in the 1990s. Positive disbelief
  in God has increased from 10% in the 1960s to 27% in the 1990s,
  showing that we are dividing more into two camps – believers and
  disbelievers – with the former less certain than they were of what
  they do believe! Part of this change comes because of pantheist theologians, of whom Teilhard de Chardin was one. Marcus Borg, the
  Hundere Distinguished Professor of Religion and Culture at Oregon
  State University, USA, is another. His book[37] distinguishes between
  God as a Spirit and as a Person. It might make a more compelling
  read if the cross of Christ was acknowledged!

Nominal Christianity

We have already touched on this above, and in the first chapter, but the
problem continues to emerge.

Matthew, the gospel of the King and the kingdom, is the only gospel
where it is recorded that people come and say, 'Lord, Lord ...' but are
excluded from the final feast.[38] These people would presumably have
called themselves members of the kingdom because they talk about the
'Lord'. They appear to be adult because of their work experience (chapter
seven), and by a comparison of their companions (chapter twenty-five).
While appearing therefore to be committed, they are in reality non-
Christian, or nominally Christian. So how do we avoid people slipping

into nominal Christianity?

The number of nominal church members is decreasing, partly because membership is no longer a convention, but also because many church members are elderly and die. They are not being replaced by younger nominal members, so younger people today are not drifting into inactive church membership (if they ever did).

At the 1998 International Lausanne Consultation on Nominalism, one paper[39] described different levels of nominality. It may be helpful to repeat these. They were:

- **ethnic-religious identity** – those whose religious commitment is closely tied to ethnic or national identity
- **second generation** – people who have distanced themselves from their parents' faith, or the faith of their parents' church
- **ritualistic** – worshippers whose outward acts of devotion are not accompanied by an inner reality of faith
- **syncretistic** – those who retain some dimensions of Christianity but have embraced aspects of spirituality and moral values from other religions or world-views
- **disillusioned** – people for whom Christianity has not worked
- **burned-out** – professional or lay people who have given all they could to the church to their own personal detriment and thus have either opted out, or remained in as a duty
- **bifurcated** – people who live dual, compartmentalised lives so that their faith is not integrated into everyday life
- **compromised** – those with a primary commitment to a spiritual, intellectual or organisational system of values which takes priority over their Christianity
- **disobedient** – those who have left the church because they are not prepared to live up to the moral standards of their particular Christian tradition
- **secularised** – people who uphold Christian values and principles without embracing Christian beliefs
- **socially distanced** – people who have never attended church regularly, but who want it to be there when they need it
- **alienated** – people who feel that they do not fit culturally or socially within the church

C S Lewis summed up the issue of nominality very neatly. 'It is only a question of using words so that we can all understand what is being said. When a man who accepts the Christian doctrine lives unworthily of it, it is much clearer to say he is a bad Christian than to say he is not a Christian.'[40]

In a Church of Scotland study on barriers to belief, one person said, 'I accept the Christian church has a job to convert people to become Christians, but I go to the Church of Scotland!'[41] This suggests the person was a nominal Christian because they had no heart to share their faith.

Spirituality

One of the elements of postmodernism that my colleague Heather Wraight teaches is that there is a 'spirituality without Christianity'. In so-called Christian Britain, this might seem almost a contradiction in terms!

Evelyn Sharpe, a consultant psychiatrist in the National Health Service, tried to evaluate the impact of the death of Diana, Princess of Wales. Among the mourners at Kensington Palace the week after her death, Sharpe found a spirituality which was neither Christian, nor one where people were expecting the church to supply a meaning. They were wanting a 'faith that gets you through the night', not one which is simplistic or irrelevant.[42] As John Drane, now Professor of Practical Theology at Aberdeen University, pointed out when speaking at a February 1998 conference called to think through the implication of the death of Diana, Princess of Wales, Paul did not disparage the spirituality he saw in Athens. He rather pointed to the altar of the unknown God, to what they knew, and declared to them Jesus.[43]

'Having been exposed to basic Christian principles at various times in their lives,' writes American researcher George Barna,[44] 'and perceiving all truth to be relative to the individual and his or her circumstances, Americans have taken to piecing together a customised version of faith that borrows liberally from any available and appealing faith.' The British are doing the same. We have 'repositioned spirituality', continues Barna. 'Faith used to revolve around God and his ordinances and principles; the faith that arrests our attention these days is that which revolves around us.'

'The problem is therefore not theological but practical. The systems, structures, institutions, and relational networks developed for the furtherance of the church are archaic, inefficient and ineffective.' John Drane takes up Barna's point: 'The way in which people handled Diana's death – particularly the underlying implied search for new self-created meta-narratives – supports the opinion that the end of our cultural love-affair with modernity has come about more on pragmatic grounds than as a result of philosophical [or theological?] principle'[45] (my brackets).

Graham Cray, Principal of Ridley Hall Theological College, has described shopping malls as the new cathedrals where people go to worship materialism on Sundays. Is it the fact that the malls are essentially pragmatic and practical that makes them attractive?

Whatever else may have happened as a consequence of the death of Diana, Princess of Wales, it has not led to any noticeable increase in church attendance, or revival, or any obvious return to God. However, did it so shake this nation that when Holy Trinity Brompton launched the national campaign encouraging attendance at Alpha courses in September 1998, the painful memory of our frailty and short life-span from a year earlier helped to invoke a much stronger and deeper response than might otherwise have come? And could the fruit of the mourning be found in those who came to faith by Alpha a year later?

Belief statistics in the general population continue to be collected and published. They have their place. It may be useful to know that 92% of Roman Catholics believe in God as opposed to 84% of those in the Church of England,[46] or that 55% believe in life after death, or that 27% pray weekly. These figures, though, do not now give us a real insight into people's spirituality.

A second phenomenon of postmodernity that my colleague lists is 'Words without meaning', and this is now the fundamental problem. What does 'God' mean? Or 'life after death'? Or 'prayer'?

Individualism

This then thrusts the argument back onto the individualism of the day and in the church. John Drane blames the churches: 'Religious institutions have lost sight of the spiritual, and therefore people need to take responsibility for their own religious quest for meaning.'[47]

Individualism may have been highlighted especially in the Thatcher years, but we are post-Thatcher now. The Berlin Wall is down, the European Union is on the rise, not least with the launch of the Euro, and Tony Blair *et al* are in the process of transforming Britain again. We have come quite a long way from Thatcher. 'Manufacturing, trade unions and the traditional family [have] waned while lawyers, supermarkets and educated waxed.'[48]

In this process we have become more open. Another facet of the Diana death was that 'people not only exposed their young children to the tragedy, but adopted their insights in seeking for resolution.'[49] Is this why church parents are willing to stop going to their church and instead find a church which their children like, and then join that? One New Church youth leader told me that three or four families were joining their church every week! Why? Because the church had an excellent teenage programme, and parents wanted their children to learn the faith, and here was a means. They recognised these parents would only be with them for five years or so, and that they would most likely then move on, but that didn't matter.

It also means that one individual's, or organisation's, standards carry weight. John Clare, Education Editor of the *Daily Telegraph*, summarising why some school inspections were successful, said, 'It is no coincidence, then, that more than one in five of the secondaries [named in the article] is, like London Oratory, a Roman Catholic school where staff, parents and pupils share a clear and highly structured view of the world. They have a ready-made ethos that other, more secular schools – the three-quarters, for example, that do not observe the law on collective worship – must strive to create for themselves.'[50]

The futurologist Dr Patrick Dixon in his book *Futurewise*,[51] feels that

Christian ethics will be a key part of Christianity that survives into the future. Change brings openness and vulnerability. Because left/right politics have all but died, he suggests the government seems to be driven by people campaigning on single issues. This is good for the church, since what most members are concerned about are single issues – such as abortion, euthanasia or human cloning.[52]

So what does all this mean?

Perhaps the implications of this chapter can be summarised as follows:

- We are increasingly living in a world where words like 'church' and 'Christian' are losing their meaning outside the lives of individuals whose personal ethics characterise them. Nominal Christians, 'bad Christians' to use C S Lewis' term, are proliferating. Commitment to individual churches is declining. People's path to faith becomes more a walk to find their own spirituality. Objective truth is scorned and with it the security it brings.
- Christianity is not 'over', it is just diluted. Attendance may decline, but loose attachment still prospers. Membership will continue to fall as will any kind of external authority, or perceived authority, which directs lifestyle, or becomes too onerous, and therefore unwanted. 'Church is good for this period of my life, but not for the next. I'm important, because I believe in me, at least at the moment.'
- It is in this sea of vagueness that churches have to operate. Those who stand firmly on objective truth will look to it for vigorous affirmation of the truths they hold dear.
- How can churches build a foundation in children's younger years which will enable them to stand when older? What is the nature of that foundation? How can truth be presented while it is being heard so that it will keep nominalism and indifference at bay later when it is not? How do we build commitment? What are the key issues and priorities the church should be addressing?

Church Ministers in the UK

There were 35,900 ministers of religion in the UK in 1995, a virtually static figure (35,700 in 1980). However, the number is slowly growing in England (by a net average of 65, or 0.2%, a year over those fifteen years) and in Northern Ireland (by one a year, or 0.05%), while it is slowly declining in Wales (by a net average loss of twenty-four a year, or 1.3%) and Scotland (by twenty-eight a year, or 0.8%).

These numbers are equivalent to 5.9 clergy per 10,000 people in England, 6.4 in Wales, 6.4 in Scotland and 11.6 in Northern Ireland, an average for the UK of 6.1 in 1995. Put another way, that means one person in every 1,630 could wear a dog collar (although the numbers include those serving full-time in denominations which do not recognise ordination). Comparative figures[1] are:

- one chartered accountant per 600 population
- one doctor per 700
- one lawyer per 1,000
- **one minister per 1,600**
- one estate agent per 1,800
- one architect per 2,100
- one dentist per 3,100

Ministers by denomination

The number of ministers naturally varies according to the size of the different denominations, but overall numbers in 1980 and 1995 are shown in Figure 8.

Figure 8: Ministers in the UK by denomination, 1980 and 1995

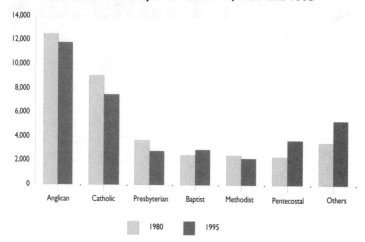

It is easy to see where the growth is – among the Baptists, Pentecostals and 'Others' (of which the main growing groups are the New Churches, Orthodox and Salvation Army). The Baptists and Salvation Army are acquiring more ministers but fewer members. The Catholics have lost the highest numbers but the Presbyterians have lost most proportionately (1.9% per year against Catholic 1.3% – Methodists by contrast are 0.7% and Anglicans 0.4%).[2]

One survey for a youth organisation showed that 28% of ministers[3] are responsible for choosing the teaching materials used in churches. Will those under increasing pressure be more likely to change the type of material being used?

Ministers by age

Most denominations do not publish the age of their clergy, but the Church of England does. The changes over twenty years are shown in Figure 9.[4]

Figure 9: Age of clergy in the Church of England, 1963 and 1983

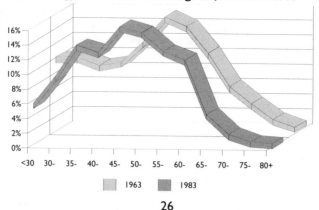

It is obvious that the trends in age over the twenty years 1963–83 have included fewer entering the ministry under thirty, and fewer staying on over sixty-five. (In 1976 the Church of England Synod introduced retirement at sixty-five in new appointments.) There are more in their thirties and forties in 1983, showing the importance of new, younger ministers.

Training colleges

There were ninety-one residential theological colleges and Bible schools in 1999 in the UK, with a total of 7,800 places, of which just over 7,200 (or 91%) were filled. The average tuition and accommodation fee was £4,100 per year. A full course lasted on average 2.5 years.[5]

However, there are pressures on the colleges. A few years ago, the Baptist Union limited the number of ministerial students each Baptist college should accept every year as there were too many students (and ministers) for churches. In at least one area, the local Methodist circuit chairman has approached the Baptist Association superintendent and asked 'if they had any ministers to spare'. Methodists 'have manse, have stipend, but no takers'.

Among the Anglican colleges, the evangelical ones have tended to be full or nearly full, the non-evangelical less so. In the mid-1990s, of the total number of ordinands in training, just over half were evangelical. The 1989 English Church Census showed that 18% of all Anglican churches were evangelical, which will probably mean that some evangelical ministers will need to serve in churches not now evangelical. Will they change their churchmanship as a consequence?

There is some criticism of colleges' syllabuses. A Church of England group within the Board of Ministry advises on the elements for a common syllabus. But other criticism relates less to the theological content than the lack of adequate leadership or management training. How are people prepared to *lead*? Many colleges have responded by introducing some suitable elements, though how far those in training can understand the nuances of leadership is less certain. Would such training be better if undertaken post-ordination? Maybe so.

Suffice to say that the content of training is under review, probably helpfully, and that in the next century, ordinands are likely to be better in tune with those they will be asked to lead.

The numbers question is more difficult to judge: how many ministers should a church have? Black churches, for instance, average 2.1 per congregation, but then both are likely to be part-time. Classic Pentecostal churches have 1.5 per church, not usually part-time. Leaving aside the Pentecostals, Free Churches generally have 0.6 ministers per congregation, the same as the Anglicans. Presbyterians have 0.5, reflecting both their shortage and the combining of responsibilities of two or more churches under a single oversight. Roman Catholics, with much larger churches, averaged 1.7 priests per church in 1995, but this fell from the 2.2

they had in 1980, again reflecting their shortage. Some dioceses, especially the Diocese of Norwich, have some clergy looking after more than ten parishes, occasionally as many as fourteen. A 1989 study showed that many clergy can cope with up to four churches, but with five or more, performance deteriorates.[6]

Length of tenure and vision

Several studies have indicated that, within limits, the longer a minister stays with his/her church, the greater likelihood of growth. Paul Beasley-Murray, now Senior Minister in a large Baptist church in Essex, in a 1981 study of half the Baptist churches in England, found that growing churches were invariably associated with ministers who had served in their current church between five and fifteen years, though some grew after over twenty-five years of service![7] The five-to-fifteen-year slot is confirmed for studies in other than Baptist churches.

Robert Schuller, who built the Crystal Cathedral in California, said in one of his books, 'Probably the foremost obstacle to church growth ... is what might best be termed "short-sighted leadership"', by which he meant pastors staying in a church for less than five years.[8] The consequence of pastors not considering long stays is that 'the average church has no ten-year plan, no fifteen-year plan, no twenty-year plan'.

The Methodist church normally moves most ministers on after five years; few of their churches are growing. The Salvation Army used to move their officers after two years; although this has now been increased to three or four or longer, few of their corps are seeing growth either.

In the USA, the average tenure of a senior pastor is four years. George Barna comments, 'In other words, many pastors must resign themselves to a life of frustration because they are changing positions before they are able to see the fruit of the early years of their administration.'[9] In other words, the frequency of their moving frustrates them because they do not see their work resulting in a growing church.

Vision can be for any length of time, of course, but most visions need to be for the subsequent five or ten years. One Anglican church which achieved real and sustained growth in Surrey in the 1980s had a minister who set ten goals for ten years of ministry. At the end of those ten years he told me, 'I have accomplished eight of these, and half-accomplished the ninth. I now know the tenth was impossible!' But his long-term vision had enabled the church to grow. A minister in a Cambridge church said, 'We don't want to change, but more families please!' Why should one come without the other?

How do the colleges train men and women to have vision? The Bible states clearly that 'where there is no vision the people perish'.[10] Where there is no vision the church perishes, where there is no vision the leader perishes, where there is no vision the people perish. Vision is crucial for ministry, and vision needs to be long term. A new method of building vision called 'Horizon Mission Methodology' is described in the final chapter.

This twenty-first century method sometimes leads to BHAGs. BHAG? It stands for 'Big Hairy Audacious Goal!'[11] A BHAG is a 'take-the-mountain' kind of challenge. Going to the moon in the 1960s was a BHAG. Building a new church hall alongside their church, and making their existing hall into an old people's home was a BHAG for one Liverpool church. 'A BHAG engages people – it reaches out and grabs them in the gut. It is tangible, energising, highly focussed. People "get it" right away; it takes little or no explanation.'[12] 'Knowing God's vision for your church' is one of the seven steps suggested by the senior pastor of a Colombian church to restoring a church to a cutting-edge ministry.[13]

Work pattern

Then there is the changing work pattern for many ministers. We have been running time management courses for many years. The key failure of those coming on them is their inability to set priorities.

The computer is an amazing machine, which most of us could not now live without, but it has not necessarily saved us precious time, especially with the advent of e-mail. 'I wish I could get my clergy away from their computers,' one bishop said to me, 'because they sit all day in front of them and think they are advancing the kingdom.' There is some, but not total, truth in this exasperated comment!

It would seem that clergy's working hours are lengthening, but there are very few measurements of it. In America Protestant ministers average sixty-five hours a week;[14] in Canada fifty-one hours, but 30% work more than sixty.[15] One UK minister in a careful analysis of his time found he worked fifty-three hours a week.[16] All those in full-time employment in the UK worked longer hours than any country in Europe in 1995 – forty-four hours a week on average, against a European standard of forty-one.[17]

'How many hours should a minister work?' I am sometimes asked. Well, if people in the UK work an average of forty-four hours, and travel to and from work plus lunch break is, say, two hours a day, then that totals fifty-four hours. A committed layman may perhaps be involved in the church for six hours a week, making a total of sixty hours. Would sixty hours be appropriate for a minister? It is true that some lay people work much longer (one study found some working people giving the church an average of two hours a day, seven days a week[18]), and it is true that some clergy work much longer than sixty hours.

The issue is less the length of hours worked, but the effectiveness of those hours. I used to have an annual medical with an ex-heart surgeon, who told me that as a surgeon he regularly worked ninety hours a week, and 'thoroughly enjoyed it'. Then he had a slight heart attack himself and, in fairness to his patients in case he had another while operating, retired to more general medical practice. I asked if he enjoyed that. 'Oh yes,' he said with enthusiasm, 'but I work less now.' How long was his average 'retired' week then? 'Never much under seventy hours,' he said! John Wesley complained when he reached eighty that he could no longer so easily work fifteen hours a day! Adlai Stevenson, the American politician, commented that 'in the long run, it is not the years in your life but the life in your years that counts'. How much do ministers enjoy their job?

One consequence of working many hours a week is that communication needs to be kept to the minimum and letters to clergy as short as possible. Allow them to ask for more information if they require it. As people contact clergy, assume that the average length of time studying their communication is likely to be at best 30 seconds.

Perhaps because of the hard work and pressures, some young people do not wish to become ministers. However, a decline in the mid-1990s in the number of ordination candidates in the Anglican theological colleges was turned around by the late 1990s, returning to the fairly constant numbers of between 400 and 450 'recommendations' per year in the 1980s,[19] but probably including more older people than those in their twenties. This may not matter too much if numbers are maintained, except that if ministers tend to attract to their churches those of similar age plus or minus ten years, then a good supply of younger ordinands would be more likely to yield more younger people at church.

The minister's place in society

On the whole, as Britain has become more secular, Christianity has become more marginalised. Such is in fact one of the measures of secularisation. As a consequence, there is scepticism about leadership,[20] both in society generally and in churches.

A group called Reform in the Church of England feels that bishops have compromised on biblical standards, especially with regard to sexuality issues. They are desiring a disestablished church, and are considering calling their own episcopal oversight, or even following the South African breakaway Church of England.[21]

There is concern that preaching is not very relevant to most of those who hear it. In a survey of 400 evangelical churchgoers across England, sermons were found to be 'of reasonable quality and moderately helpful but nearly 50% said that the preaching and teaching were marked by lack of relevance, depth or challenge'.[22] In one of his last addresses, Bishop Lesslie Newbigin said he was 'horrified by the extent to which so much of the preaching that goes on in the church is about the context, not about the text .... For me, what you become depends on what you attend to.'[23] He went on to talk about his personal Bible reading time every morning. The areas of greatest concern about the church voiced by respondents to an article in the magazine of the

National Council for Christian Standards was 'lack of preaching God's Word in Spirit and in truth, and failure to proclaim a clear gospel message'.[24]

The church's place in society

The church's place in society is inextricably bound up with its ministerial leadership. In Northern Ireland, for example, in the 1990s the church was playing an important part in the peace process. 'The lack of grace is doing great damage,' said one observer at a private function. 'The church leaders responded self-righteously to the eventual peace package on Good Friday. They didn't like it, but they couldn't deliver anything better. So why, if the churches can't come up with joint programmes for action, should they be allowed to join Civic Forums?'

'The church is in danger of forfeiting the respect of the nation by becoming over-accommodating towards society,' said Luis Palau in his East Midlands mission in October 1998.[25] In a sermon at his former parish of All Saints in central London in November 1998, Archbishop David Hope said the church was 'dull, pedestrian, committee-speak and committee-bound, utilitarian ... was becoming issue-driven and exclusive',[26] and therefore increasingly irrelevant for many people. Then a parish priest, Robin Gamble, in his book *The Irrelevant Church*,[27] focused on how the working class felt alienated from traditional Christianity. Now it is not just the working class! Some people are put off by their own image of the church. 'For many people, church is such a sacred place, they don't feel good enough to get through the door.'[28] But 'abandoning the institutional church to retire into a "private world of faith" won't help those who are frustrated with the church', said Dr George Carey in Paris at the 1998 annual conference of the Anglican Institute.[29]

When asked why he wrote his book *Struggling to Belong*, Simon Jones said, 'So many people struggle with the church. They complain it is unwelcoming, arrogant, unreal and prone to chop life into handy little compartments. We dismiss the complaints saying that unbelievers can't be expected to grasp what church is about. The trouble is, it's Christians who are talking.'[30] And perhaps especially young people. But it's not only young people. Older people are showing their tiredness with the church by simply turning up less often. Frequency of attendance is a big issue, and was mentioned in the previous chapter.

But this comes at a time when breakfast TV star Johnny Vaughan converted to Catholicism when he got married in 1999. He found Christianity while in jail for selling drugs.[31] The actor Mel Gibson returned to the Catholic church. *She* magazine said, 'It has become cool to be Christian' because people in their 30s 'are seeing their parents get older, they worry about the future for their children and are returning to the church'.[32]

David Edwards, former Provost of Southwark Cathedral, sums it up well when he says, 'The churches will have to find their own places in a society which is pluralist in its irreversible nature, and the leaders of the churches will have to find their own roles in religious communities which share at least something of the general scepticism about leaders. The churches will be free but in a free society; their leaders will be entitled to appeal to consciences but their members will persist in making their own decisions according to their own consciences.'[33]

Leadership

What then is the leadership towards which a minister should aspire? It varies. A study of members of the Christian Research Association found that not every minister is a leader. Perhaps one in three, 31%, had the gifts of leadership as defined by the management consultant Meredith Belbin,[34] double the proportion in an earlier study among Anglican clergy in the Diocese of Bradford (18%).[35] But the fact that two-thirds or more of ministers in these samples were still in positions of leadership meant that they had to exercise the gift of leadership from a position where it was not their primary gifting, that is, not their strongest point. It is likely that both samples are biased, but it is likely to be true that the majority of actual church leaders do not have a primary gifting of leadership! George Barna also concludes, 'Most senior pastors serving churches today are not truly leaders, although they hold a position of leadership.'[36]

What kind of leadership is required? To some extent that varies according to size of church, and the management characteristics of that size:

Table 4: Management styles in a church

Size	Style	Implications of that style
Under 50	Supervisor	Delegates but retains decision responsibility. Dependency culture
50–199	Junior management	Some delegation but church revolves around one (full-time) person — a multi-talented generalist
200–349	Middle management	Delegation of authority; leader provides support
350–599	Top management	A growing ministry team; full-time professionals rather than part-time volunteers
600 or over	Chairman of Board	Highly complex management structure

Just think of the different management styles operated by people like Colin Dye of Kensington Temple, Richard Bewes of All Souls, Langham Place, Sandy Millar of Holy Trinity Brompton, R T Kendall at Westminster Chapel, Ben Davies at Bracknell Family Centre, Nigel Wright at Altrincham Baptist Church. They are all effectively operating as 'Chairmen of Boards'; how do they compare with, say, John Harvey Jones of ICI, or even Tony Blair – not in what they do, but in how they do it? Bishop Gavin Reid said at the memorial service of Morgan Derham, former General Secretary of the Evangelical Alliance, that he had 'never

[been] afraid to pioneer in areas where the evangelicals of his day had feared to tread.'[37]

A minister by him/herself typically cannot take a church to above about 200 people. David Wasdell, then of the Urban Church Project, showed in a 1974 analysis of Anglican churches and the number of incumbents and curates that one full-time minister can relate to about 150-200 people. This is why so many churches find it difficult to grow beyond 200. One person normally has a maximum acquaintance of 168 people whose names can be recalled quickly.

The '200 factor' is not just Anglican-related; it is true for all non-Catholic denominations. One Methodist minister was asked to be responsible for two churches, one with a congregation of 150 and one with sixty-five. He found he literally could not do it – the 200 factor came into play. It is not essential that the second person to help is an ordained minister: any other full-time person will do – a secretary, youth worker, sometimes a music director or social worker. And the second person needs to be brought in *before* the church grows, not after – in fact, it won't happen afterwards. As any hard-pressed minister of a busy church will tell you, if the church is to break the 200 barrier, more staff are essential now!

So what do we do?

Richard Higginson, Director of the Ridley Hall Foundation for the Study of Faith and Works Issues, believes the more successful commercial companies are moving into the so-called 'third wave'. Such companies create markets, focus on the individual, are open to change, are more flexible, interdependent, inspirational, allow personal growth, provide information, and make a difference to the world, seeking to build for the future. He says 'third wave companies are the emerging form … for all institutions.'[38] This might be summed up in the words of one satirical journalist about current politicians, 'Britain will benefit if the next generation of leaders learns to think for others as well as itself.'[39]

Richard Higginson firmly places leadership in the aligning and inspiring mode. Leadership means knowing what the next step is. He quotes Warren Bennis, the American author of two influential books on leadership:

- the manager has a short-range view; the leader has a long-term perspective
- the manager has his eye always on the bottom line; the leader has his eye on the horizon
- managers are people who do things right; leaders are people who do the right thing[40]

33

What might frustrate such lofty aspirations to leadership? He suggests: a yearning for power; doing the right thing for the wrong reason; wanting to be noticed; the desire to be popular with everyone; avoiding conflict at all costs; dwelling on one's inadequacies; interpreting everything as an attack on oneself.[41] He points out that these can be just as true for church leaders as secular leaders.

What more then shall we say? The importance of good leadership is unquestioned. What is good leadership? There are many definitions. Let the words of Warren Bennis, the management guru, conclude this chapter. He says that effective leaders:

- have a strong sense of purpose, a passion, a conviction for wanting to do something important
- are capable of developing and sustaining deep and trusting relationships
- are purveyors of hope and have positive illusions about reality
- have a balance in their lives between work, power and family or outside activities
- have a bias toward action and, while not reckless, do not resist taking risks[42]

Part of the problem is not knowing what to do. Leadership has its own set of burdens and pressures, and can be very lonely.[43] Often leaders are marginalised. Ministers' preaching is often not as relevant as it might be. People in positions of leadership are often used by others for their own selfish ends, and are often looked upon as role models, even when they do not want to be seen in that way.[44]

Should self-assessment be encouraged? Paul Hills, Baptist Union Superintendent of the Eastern Area, has prepared an excellent set of forms to help evaluation of the church generally, and then its worship, preaching, spirituality, community, mission and resources.[45]

Should ministerial self-discipline be encouraged? But then nearly half of bosses take work away with them on holiday and only 43% take a full five-week entitlement.[46] How far should one encourage ministers to do the same? Is *enjoying* the job really at least half the key?

Is helping churches get vision the key? Or helping churches move to cutting-edge ministries? What will be different in the churches in the UK in 2010 as a consequence of what we do in the next two years?

Church and
Young People

We talk about 'boomers' and 'busters' as if we all knew what these terms meant, and as if we all carried in our heads their demographic profile. The Americans had their population boom (where the word 'boomers' comes from) in the late 1940s and 1950s, whereas in the UK this occurred about ten years later, largely because of the huge number of especially Irish immigrants in the late 1950s. But their way of defining the age group allows us to use their categorisations and the years to which they relate without having to alter them. Strictly speaking, we should include 1965 in the British 'boomers', as that year witnessed a peak in the number of births, that is, it was the height of the British baby boom.

Builders (aged 55–73 in 2000)
'Builders' are so-called because they helped to rebuild the world after the Second World War, re-establishing the economic and social systems we use today. They were the parents of the...

Boomers (aged 36–54 in 2000)
These are marginally the largest 'generation' in the UK population. Terry Green, Chief Executive of Debenhams, explained what they meant to him in an interview: 'They have seen the 1970s and what that brought: the three-day week and the misery. They have seen the boom of the 1980s. Now in the 1990s they have been through recession, seen what that involves, and they are a lot wiser. They are not stupid; they have a sensitivity that is not readily understood by many people.'[1] Of course, the older generations have lived through the 1970s and 1980s too; the 'boomers' cannot be said to be uniquely experienced or sensitive.

Busters (aged 17–35 in 2000)
A lively article[2] summarised a Commencement Address given by Australian Rowland Croucher at the University of Queensland in March 1998. He described 'busters' (those who broke through, or 'bust', the boom), or Generation Xers, as:

- survivors of the most aborted generation in history
- the best educated, most travelled and longest-living generation ever
- the first to grow up with AIDS, MTV and environmental catastrophes
- the first electronic generation, having already mastered laptops, the Internet, CD-Roms, faxes, modems, Nintendo, Sega and PlayStation (They have a tremendous ability to process lots of information at once. Playing video games while talking on the phone, listening to the radio, doing their homework and making a snack was an after-school ritual for this generation. This 'parallel thinking' allows 'multiple tasking'.)
- the first generation to be raised completely by TV (so 'everything is image') and shaped by music: and their lyrics are often passionate and angry, sometimes rebellious, mostly honest, sometimes spiritual/religious (There's a pervasive longing for reality, healing, community and peace. One GenXer said, 'Music is our lifeblood – I'd rather buy music than eat.' And they would rather be at a U2 concert than in church singing hymns.)
- anti-materialistic (So they'll have a succession of jobs, rather than a career. And they'll put relationships before work – work is what you do so that you can have a life.)
- having insatiable appetites for junk food, junk films, junk ideas and junk culture
- rejecting institutions (This is a collaborative generation – hierarchies are 'out.')
- needing the church more than any other generation and wanting it so little (Although they are 'spiritual', they know less about the Bible than any previous generation in the past 1,000 years.)
- the first 'latch-key' generation, with many of them coming from two-job families
- affirming diversity and being able to live with ambiguity
- fewer than half of them has lived with two biological parents throughout their childhood
- the first generation to grow up without absolute truths, believing that the highest virtue is tolerance of the views of others – post-Christian and postmodern

Lowell Sheppard, former National Director of Youth For Christ in the UK, but now living in Japan, says a 'new church is required to reach the new young. It will emphasise the following:

- creativity and encouragement of individual expression
- relevant and applied teaching of scripture
- affirmation and encouragement of spiritual experiences and demonstrations of supernatural power
- involvement in holistic mission
- small and large groups to which the new young can belong'[3]

The Mosaics (aged 0–17 in 2000)

The age of their teachers is important because their attitude to teaching will vary, and their thinking will be different from the young people's. How far, for example, will the 'mosaics' fit into the above pattern for 'busters'? How far will 'buster' type of thinking make children more or less receptive to the biblical story? Many such kinds of questions can be asked.

They are relevant if the differences, especially the conceptual differences of the way the different generations learn, is noted. For example, 'builders' and 'boomers' were largely trained to think in a linear logical way. 'Mosaics' think 'mosaicly' (where the term comes from), that is, in a kind of crossword patchwork, or putting together a mosaic of Roman tessellated tiles, getting a bit of the picture here and another bit there.

The difference may be seen perhaps in the teaching of history. 'Builders' were taught history, especially English history, across centuries. The school I went to in the 1950s covered 1066 to 1914. This is not how history is taught today. Certain people or periods may be focused on, such as Cromwell, or the Victorian era. The concerns, or principles, of the period would be established. Thus trend thinking is less frequent, and the picture of history is built up as a jigsaw rather than a continuous story. Churchill's *History of the English Speaking Peoples* is not a textbook title today. A number of books have been written exploring these changes in a Christian context.[4]

Another element in the generational variations is the importance of relationship between grandparent and grandchildren. One study showed that the family which prays together really does stay together, with churchgoing grandparents more likely to be close to their grandchildren than non-churchgoers.[5] However, another found that children had 10% less contact with grandparents in 1998 than they did in 1988.[6] Increased geographical distance is partly to blame, but this is not the whole reason; there was also less contact by telephone.

Generational variations

Table 5 gives a broad overview of these categories,[7] and introduces thereby the latest one. A sixth has been added, with a title I have made up, but which reflects the fact that the next generation will not look at one picture as in a Roman mosaic, but rather a moving mix of pictures, all made of the same parts. Just as the 'mosaics' have been called Generation Y, as the children of Generation X, so it is likely that their next generation will be called Generation Z. Whatever their title, we simply cannot ignore the next generation. How will they differ from the latest one?

Table 5: Six generations of British people

Generation	Years of birth	Age range in 2000	Population size (estimated 2001)
Seniors	1926 and earlier	74 +	4.5 million
Builders[1]	1927-45	55 to 73	12.4 million
Boomers	1946-64	36 to 54	15.1 million
Busters[2]	1965-83	17 to 35	14.6 million
Mosaics[3]	1984-02	Up to 16	12.6 million
Kaleidoscopes	2003-21	To be born!	0 million

[1] Also called Boosters or the Maturity Generation in some literature

[2] Also called Generation X or Friends in some literature

[3] Also called Beepers (because they have grown up in the IT age), the Millennium Generation, Generation Y, or Thatcher's Children in some literature, especially British

What do the differences between these groups mean? One helpful description of the middle three was published in *Too Valuable to Lose*[8] which related specifically to mission work. It is reproduced below as an example of the major differences between these groups:

Table 6: A three-generation perspective on mission issues

Issue	Builders	Boomers	Busters
Call	Mystical	Best job fit	'Best' mission: often the most caring
Focus of commitment	Particular people or country with particular mission organisation	Ministry in which and wherever gifts are best used	Particular project
Length of commitment	Life	Short term and review	Short term
Attitude to mission agency	High loyalty	Low loyalty	Low loyalty
Leadership	Authoritarian; respect status	Participatory, consensus; respect competence	Participatory team; respect genuineness and openness
Approach to conflict	Indirect or denial	Clarify and work towards reconciliation	Direct, open and honest
Attitude to support and pastoral care	Independent	Expect opportunity for both; willing to try and see	Perceive both as essential to well-being
Role issues	Generalists; prepared to do anything; make do	Specialists; pursue excellence; agents of change	Function best in teams, each with focussed ministry
Wives' roles	Supporting husband	Contribution in own right	Prefer husband-wife team; egalitarian marriage
Devotional life	No Bible, no breakfast	Wherever it can be fitted in	Find discipline hard but long for spiritual things
Relationship to local community	Paternalistic	Fraternalistic	Work well under church

'Mosaics' have not been involved yet in sufficient depth for a further column of boxes for them in Table 6. But some could be filled in, like 'Call – Can you give me a job?'; 'Focus of commitment – what I like doing'. Many of the boxes will, as yet, still be the same as for 'busters'.

Infant baptism

In each of 1993, 1994 and 1995 exactly half, 50%, of babies were baptised in the first year of life (with the exception of a small number who were baptised as children but between the ages of one and twelve). In 1996 this percentage dropped to 49%, but the size of the percentage shows the importance of this rite of passage.

For some, it is a meaningful dedication of their child to God. Others see the service as bringing the child into a covenant relationship with God, dependent on the promises made by parents and godparents. Others however see it differently.

In some research we undertook for the Church of Scotland, we asked a number of adults who said they were Christians but who did not attend church frequently if they would have their babies baptised. The answer was a uniform yes. Did they think it reasonable for the minister to suggest they attend the church for a few weeks beforehand so that they could get used to the church? No, they did not – what had the church attendance of the parent got to do with the baptism of the child?

Was it reasonable for the minister to ask if they believed in God before undertaking the baptism? Again, no – what does the parents' faith have to do with a child's baptism? In some desperation, we then asked what did they think baptism did to the child? The answer was that 'it puts the child into the eye of God'. This is essentially a pagan belief: undergoing an appropriate ritual to invoke the god's blessing.

The massive difference between the 50% baptised and the 6% of the child population in Sunday School demonstrates that there is no meaningful relation between the two. Might it be worth trying somehow to make the link more explicit? Some special kind of infant baptism follow-up perhaps?

Does baptism lead to confirmation in Anglican churches? Confirmation may be at any mature age, but most confirmations take place in the teen years. Taking fifteen as an average age (the actual average is not known), what percentage are confirmations of baptisms fifteen years earlier in the Church of England? Between 1900 and 1925 the percentage averaged 38%; between 1925 and 1950 it dropped to 36%, and then between 1950 and 1970 rose to 37%, a remarkably even proportion for the first seventy years of the century. Since 1970, however, it dropped to 23% over just a decade.[9]

The Church of England has experimented with allowing some parishes to give communion to children before they are confirmed, and has found that many more of those children stayed on in church in their teenage years than might otherwise have been expected to do so.[10] However, some object theologically to this practice.[11]

Sunday School

In 1989 the English Church Census showed that 82% of Free Church children and 64% of Anglican children attended Sunday School, a total of almost 600,000 children.[12] The trends in the 1990s and the early results of the 1998 *English Church Attendance Survey* suggest that that figure was much lower a decade later. Professor David Martin, formerly of the LSE, estimated that 'in 1957, 76% of those aged over thirty had at some time attended Sunday School.'[13] In 1992 the proportion was down to 41%, many of whom would be over fifty. By 2002 the proportion will be 33%, of whom perhaps 80% will be over sixty. Dave Roberts, editor of *Renewal* magazine, has argued that in the 1950s when knowledge of Bible stories was so much greater, people needed to be taken from 'knowledge to commitment'.[14] He continues, 'We have literally millions of children now who don't even have the knowledge.'

The peak of Sunday School attendance was in 1905 when the churches collectively looked after 56% of the child population in Sunday School, teaching them the three Rs, and a fourth R, Religion, or rather, Christianity. The percentage has declined steadily since then.[15] 'Although Sunday School was originally conceived as a way of teaching people both reading skills and Biblical principles, today's churches are doing little to stem the decline in literacy and have failed to adopt new means of effective communication.'[16]

Figure 10 shows the changing percentage of children attending Sunday School between 1985 and 1989 by denomination, and Figure 11 the combined percentage by English region.

Figure 10: Proportions of children in Sunday School by denomination, 1985 and 1989

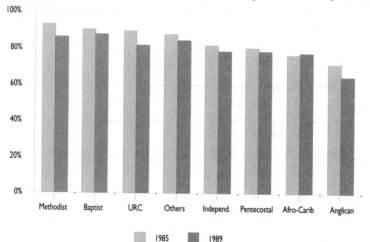

Figure 11: Proportions of children in Sunday School by region, 1985 and 1989

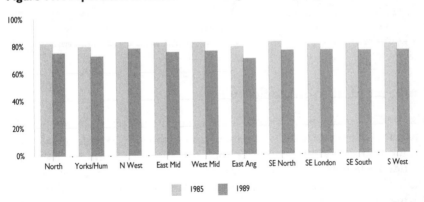

These two diagrams show that there is more variation by denomination than by part of the country.

'Sunday Schools are in crisis,' claimed Ruth Gledhill, the *Times* Religious Correspondent, in an article in January 1998. Martin Lambourne, Director of Resource Development at the National Children's Education Council, says 'The truth is, the Sunday School movement, as a distinct movement, died with the advent of the Family Church in the 1960s.'[17] A couple in their eighties wrote to us, 'There is great concern for the Sunday School. Numbers are very small. It doesn't help the situation that there is no one who will accept the overall responsibility, so a group of half a dozen or so take it in turn to teach the children, week by week.'

A detailed analysis of Baptists in Scotland[18] observed that 'in the past, church membership figures were dependent on the numbers in Sunday School a decade earlier, whereas now the dependency is the other way (Sunday School numbers depend on church membership levels)'. In other words, in the first half of the twentieth century, those coming to Sunday School broadly remained with the church; in the latter half, this doesn't happen, and Sunday School depends on the family status of the adults present in church (that is, do those coming bring their children?).

The obvious deduction is that we should win the adults and the children will then automatically come. Dave Roberts in the earlier cited article[19] would disagree: we must seek the children for their own sake. There is also the confusion that far fewer young people wish to take out membership of a church than was the case fifty to eighty years ago.

In a lecture on 'The Age of Information', Alan Rogers, then Head of BBC Television: Education, commenting on children in Sunday School 'updated to Junior Church', said, 'Is the stress on learning or on belonging? Is learning really happening, or is it a matter of child-minding – and never mind about being too tough, because the children might choose not to come back. One has the greatest sympathy. Children tend to drop out of church from the age when they could really get down to some serious learning about Christianity. But is this good enough?'[20]

A couple who had been missionaries in Mozambique wrote to our office, saying, 'Children seem to miss out so much these days: little or no Bible teaching in school, few brought to Sunday School, less and less Bible in the media. Without overt persecution we can still become a godless society.'[21]

Enjoyment of Sunday School

The 1992 *Reaching and Keeping Teenagers* survey asked teenagers both in churches (who were mostly Christian) and schools (who were mostly not) if they had attended Sunday School. Of the school sample, 34% had attended when they were five or six, as against 57% of the church sample. Similar proportions held when they were nine or ten, but when they were thirteen or fourteen, only 12% in school but 55% in church attended.[22] How much did they enjoy it? Their reactions are reproduced in Table 7. The church answers were also analysed by churchmanship, and these answers, a sub-division of the church column, are given after the overall figures to save confusion:

Table 7: Reactions to Sunday School

Reaction	School %	Church %	Overall %	Evangelical %	Non-evangelical %
'Enjoyable'	37	64	52	70	55
'An opportunity to learn a lot'	29	51	41	57	40
'An encouragement to attend church'	22	42	33	45	36
'Boring'	32	17	24	16	19
'A waste of time'	27	6	15	6	6
'Irrelevant'	13	7	10	6	8
Total number (=100%)	589	755	1,344	447	298

Over half the children enjoyed Sunday School, two-thirds in the church sample, rather more evangelicals than non-evangelicals. Half the church teenagers found Sunday a learning expierence, again evangelical more so than non-evangelicals. On the negative side, a third of the school sample but only a sixth of the church sample found Sunday School boring.

What makes Sunday School enjoyable? Relationship-building activities would seem to be part of the enjoyable elements, as well as being a 'buster' characteristic (see Table 6).

John Drane has said that telling stories was part of the way people explored spirituality in the aftermath of the death of Diana, Princess of Wales.[23] This is also part of a 'buster's' world-view, so the telling of *The Greatest Story Ever Told*, as Hollywood dubbed the Bible, is an important way of communicating the faith. The methodology of telling stories could add to the enjoyment of Sunday School because of the appropriateness of the format. This is perhaps particularly seen in the very popular and highly praised Holiday Clubs that Scripture Union and others encourage. As young people become conscious of the emptiness of materialism (as many do), the absence of exposure to Christianity makes them more genuinely open to its story, especially the Old Testament story.[24]

One very enjoyable type of Sunday School that I personally observed one week in a local church was that called Kids' Church, which is supported by the American *Charisma* materials. There was a huge amount of preparation to do every week, and the activities involved included acting, playing games, watching a video, puppets, listening to stories, etc, in a non-stop session for sixty to seventy-five minutes. The *modus operandi* changed every six to eight minutes, and employed 'mosaic' thinking as its basis. Very biblical, highly original in many ways, but exhausting for the adults! The children, however, love it and come back week after week for more.

There is, however, a great danger in enjoyable Sunday Schools. One person we interviewed succinctly summed it up when she said, 'People today want children to be happy, not good'. We can so emphasise the first, that we overlook the second.

Leaving Sunday School

The *Reaching and Keeping Teenagers* survey also found that, if children were going to leave Sunday School, they stayed for about four years before they left. What might they be expected to be taught in that time? When we asked ministers that question, the answer varied according to churchmanship. Evangelicals wanted to give both the opportunity to respond to the gospel as well as a broad range of biblical knowledge (both Old and New Testaments); non-evangelicals wanted to offer a faith opportunity but favoured a smaller range of biblical material (mostly New Testament).

The Sunday School lesson also has to be relevant, the lack of which attribute may have caused teenagers to say it was 'boring' rather than the more sophisticated evaluation of 'irrelevant'. Rev Alister McGrath, Principal of Wycliffe Hall, an evangelical college, says, 'Above all, we need to take the trouble to relate the message to its audience, making sure that it scratches where people itch.[25] The difficulty with poor Sunday Schools is that there is now a generation with some church experience who are currently outside the church and don't wish to return. 'We've tried it already,' they say.

Philip Richter and Leslie Francis, respectively Methodist and Anglican educational researchers, in an important study of why people leave church, *Gone but not Forgotten*,[26] analysed the material by whether the respondents were over or under 20. The reasons for leaving were similar for both age groups (in order – unfulfilled expectations, changes in life circumstances, and loss of faith), but there was one area where there was a difference. This is what the authors call 'stage of faith' and is a reference to the work on faith development[27] by Professor James Fowler of the Center for Research in Faith and Moral Development at Emory University in Atlanta, USA. He diagnosed six stages of faith and analysed these by age group. Using titles adapted from another book:[28]

- stage one: impressionistic faith (early childhood)
- stage two: ordering faith (childhood or beyond)
- stage three: conforming faith (adolescence and beyond)
- stage four: choosing faith (young adulthood and beyond)
- stage five: balanced faith (early mid-life and beyond)
- stage six: selfless faith (mid-life and beyond)

If people are leaving before the age of twenty for faith-stage reasons, this suggests that they do so as they begin to move from stage three to stage four, because the majority of teenagers are in stage three and those in their twenties in stage four. It could simply be that the cost of discipleship, or a realisation of the implications of what the Christian life involves, causes some to leave. This parallels the findings of the survey of why people leave church by Eddie Gibbs, Professor of Church Growth at Fuller Theological Seminary, Los Angeles.[29]

Teachers and Sunday School parents

The relationship between the Sunday School teacher and the parents and families of the children taught has weakened in many Sunday Schools today. In the past, parents and teacher knew each other personally, and some Sunday School teachers even made an annual or quarterly visit to the child's home. Today teachers rarely have the time, and even if they did, they would not always be welcome. Parents are pressured also, especially if both are working.

Likewise, pupils were sometimes asked to tea by their teacher, perhaps in ones or twos. Such opportunities built up the relationship between teacher and pupil and allowed for personal spiritual conversations.

Those kinds of relationships are very rare today. But are there other actions which could be taken to build up these key relationships? For example, what about an 'Open Evening' (like a day school parents' evening) for parents of Sunday School children?

The need for good relationships isn't confined to teachers and parents; they are important for the children themselves. The National Curriculum focuses on subjects like mathematics and language skills, which can be tested and evaluated. 'Soft skills' relating to interpersonal behaviour can be neglected because they are less measurable and less valid as educational foci. 'As a result, students are less comfortable and less well prepared to engage in relationship building, listening, conflict resolution, negotiating, team building, and creative problem solving,' wrote one observer of the American scene,[30] evaluating the lack of soft skills she observed. Is the same true in the UK? If so, is this an area in which the Sunday School could help more? A *Reader's Digest* poll in 1994 found that nearly nine parents in ten wanted children to be taught right from wrong.[31] A similar proportion might welcome children being helped with relationships.

Teaching in Sunday School

The responses to interviews with ministers for some youth research were quite grim in some respects. They acknowledged:

1 **Fewer people wished to teach in Sunday School for various reasons:**
   - They attended church less than weekly and wished to go to church rather than teach when they did turn up.
   - They knew they didn't know how to teach in today's teaching culture, or how to control noisy children.
   - They didn't know their Christian faith well enough to be able to answer the children's questions.
   - Those who did teach wanted to stop being a teacher after a relatively short time: less commitment is how most ministers view this.
   - Many teachers now teach on a rota system, so are actually with the children less frequently.

2 **Children appear less regularly:**
   - This meant that preparation was difficult: one teacher we spoke to had six children one week and 25 the next.
   - They were not always brought by parents, but sometimes by grandparents or neighbours, so getting to know the family was less straightforward.
   - It also meant that the children didn't necessarily know each other very well.
   - As well as decreasing frequency of visits, there are also fewer children in total coming in many churches.

3 **Lessons are less easy to prepare:**
   - The way children are taught today is different from the way that many of the teachers themselves were taught.
   - Children learn differently – and take in information at a faster rate than older adults.
   - Children think differently from adults – 'mosaicly' not 'linearly'. This means they tune out after six to eight minutes unless a transition catches their interest.
   - They have far, far less Bible knowledge so need to be given much more background detail.
   - The words being used to teach must be less theological, judgemental or paternalistic.
   - There is the constant need to use more technology, if only because children very often attribute greater truth to a technological source of

information than they do to a person,[32] and also because they are steeped in technology at home and at day school.

4 Teaching materials may change:
- Individual teachers sometimes now are allowed to choose what teaching material they wish to use. This sometimes means that more than one type is used within the same Sunday School – hence the need to market to each individual Sunday School teacher if possible!
- Whichever system is used, the pressure is to change it every so often just because 'it's good to have a change'.
- Some Sunday Schools wish to have lectionary-based materials; others don't.
- Teaching materials need to include information on *how to teach* the Bible as well as *what to teach* from the Bible.
- Teaching materials may not assume that other Christian-related activities, like Bible-reading, will necessarily be pursued.
- Only 49% of churches encourage children to read the Bible.[33]

Competition

There are now more alternative activities available on Sundays than previously, such as sporting events, musical festivals and shopping. Additionally, families (including Christian families) think of Sundays as visiting days, and for split families, Sunday can be 'Daddy's day'.

As a consequence, some churches are moving Sunday School to a week-night, where it becomes 'Wednesday School' or whatever. However, it can then compete with other youth activities run by the church or others, including uniformed organisations.

Conversely, uniformed organisations and other youth activities may transfer their work to a Sunday in order to attract larger numbers. This also means a possible conflict with Sunday School.

Behind such changes are the issues of priorities, and behind priorities lies overall church strategy. But many churches don't have a youth strategy (or any other!). How can the ministers and leaders be helped to shape a strategic plan for their church for the next, say, five years?

Numbers attending church services

A survey for one youth organisation showed that 77% of children attended the morning adult service of churches for at least part of the time. There is also the evidence from the 1989 English Church Census that 20% of English children (those under fifteen) attended the adult service for the *entire* time in 1985, rising to 26% by 1989. But the reasons for this begin to emerge from the changing face of family involvement in church and the frequency with which parents attend, and the familiarity of children with a Sunday School they may only occasionally attend. This will be covered in greater depth in the next chapter.

Adult baptism

The Baptist Union keeps records of the number of adult baptisms but not the age of those baptisms, although many will be of teenagers. The Baptist Unions of both Great Britain and Scotland can correlate the number of baptisms with significant evangelistic events, like Billy Graham's Harringay Crusade in 1954, or the 1989 three-city Livelink Mission in Scotland. They have also found that after five years, 69% of those baptised are still worshipping in the same church regularly,[34] and presumably others are still attending if in different churches.

Does this high percentage suggest that adult baptism is a more meaningful expression of personal faith, and therefore more likely to encourage continued commitment to the Christian faith? There is of course a theological issue here as well as a pragmatic one!

Church developments

In addition to the above challenges at youth level, there is a further challenge at church level. This may show itself in one of two ways, it would seem.

Firstly, there is a movement, especially in New Churches (and all New Frontiers churches) to move towards a cell church type structure, in which the congregation is split into units of perhaps a dozen people for worship and teaching. These are, however, also evangelistic and have the aim of growing larger and then subdividing. The danger is that as families come together for worship, the dominant types of teaching are adult, with less room for specific children's activity. Even when undertaken, unless in a specific children's cell, there will be just two or three children in a group and a programme such as given in traditional Sunday School teaching materials would be inappropriate. Maybe in such a cell, a sixteen-year old will teach an eight-year old.

There are examples where the cell group structure works well, such as Blomvlei Road Baptist Church in Cape Town, South Africa, which has 250 people in twenty-five cells, five of which are children's cells, held in the afternoon or early evening. They also continue to have central Sunday services, and their Sunday attendance has increased from 300 to 500. Seventy-five members have opted out of cells; the rest are not yet linked up.[35] Experience of cells is still new.

Secondly, many churches are failing to grow, and are growing older in outlook as a consequence. These fail to attract young people, and increasingly lack the resources for attracting young people. Some people, like the Rev Robert Warren, Church of England Officer for the Decade of Evangelism, feel that larger churches 'are typically static, ageing and heading towards decline.'[36]

There is some truth in both these factors. There is no question that church congregations are ageing and that the proportion of Sunday attenders aged under fifteen has shrunk drastically since the late 1980s. This is discussed in more detail in *The Tide is Running Out*,[37] giving the results of the 1998 *English Church Attendance Survey*, from which the following bar-chart is extracted:

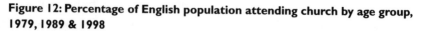

Figure 12: Percentage of English population attending church by age group, 1979, 1989 & 1998

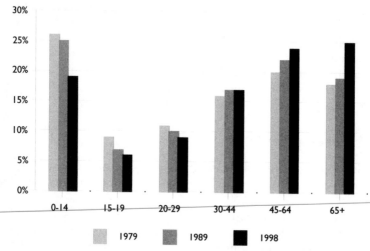

This shows a very serious drop in attendance among the under-fifteens. The proportion aged thirty to forty-four has remained unaltered – this is broadly the age group when many couples start their families, or have children not yet old enough to leave home. But with smaller families, and more split families, plus competition from other activities on Sundays, they are bringing fewer children with them to church.

One youth leader said to me that some organisations train youth workers for evangelism, but do not train them on how to keep young people. This was the concern of Lowell Sheppard, former National Director of Youth For Christ, who realised the urgency of keeping, as well as reaching, young people.

Age of conversion

The average age of conversion was 14 years 9 months (the younger teenager) in 1968;[38] in 1994, it had risen to 18 years 11 months[39] (the older teenager). In 1968, 76% of all those who came to faith did so by the age of twenty; in 1994, it had fallen to 70%. Although the average age is increasing and the proportions converted under the age of twenty is decreasing, both these trends are slow. For many years into the twenty-first century, the majority of conversions will still occur before young people reach twenty years of age. Hence the importance of going all out to reach them.

Drift from the churches

In an important book under this title,[40] William Kay and Leslie Francis present a coherent summary of their extensive research into attitudes towards Christianity during childhood and adolescence, as well as taking note of relevant research from other sources. Ranging over a variety of social and psychological factors, they see a continuing drift away from the church, both as pupils get older (ie, the drift is more pronounced in secondary than primary school) and over time, since 1970. They also note that the trend has intensified recently.

They posit a number of factors: the social and contextual influences of home, father's occupation (or social class) and school, the individual influences of age, gender and personality (with the third a key component of the second of those), and the moral influence of a hardening attitude towards others, an eroding attitude towards self and the abandonment of traditional moral values.

Church schools can make a significant contribution to the development of a positive attitude towards Christianity among their pupils, but not all do so. However, pupils who have lapsed from their Christian faith, or are of a denomination other than that of the school they attend, can undermine the spiritual impact of the school as a whole.

Pupils who follow an RE syllabus which concentrates on world religions are much less likely to have a positive attitude to Christianity than those whose syllabus concentrates on Christianity and the Bible. Pupils who have a personal religious experience are more likely to be positive to Christianity than those who haven't. Scientism (an excessive belief in, or application of scientific method) rather than science itself, militates against Christianity as does the conflict between different accounts of human origins.

Other developments

One of the key concerns of young people, both in Europe and in the UK, is their future employment. In a 1997 survey, 76% of young people felt that getting people work should be top priority for the European Union.[41] Somehow a theology of work needs to be developed in the minds of young Christians.

Young people are increasingly computer-literate. The same survey found that 43% used a computer regularly. As the technological capability of the computer increases, along with the Internet, young people will increasingly become moulded by this medium. The challenge to the church is how to use it to advance biblical teaching in the best way possible.

At a seminar in April 1992, the Finnish Director of Research for the *European Values Systems Study* spoke about the new societal values being developed in Europe. He highlighted these as:

- creative security (as against the old economic and social security)
- independence (as against community)
- new soft technologies (as against old hard ones)
- self-authority (as against delegated or positioned authority)

He also indicated that moral attitudes were leading on the one hand to a more tolerant position (people must be allowed to believe/live however they choose), but also an increasingly intolerant position (no one's going to stand in the way of *my* rights to self-determination).

So where does all this take us?

It is clear that the goalposts for children's work have changed drastically, and the children themselves have changed also. And this changing process is continuing. Sunday School has an honourable history, but the institution needs renewal. It is still vital to reach young people with the gospel. This is still the most responsive period of their lives. What shape should that renewal take? Perhaps we should consider the following features:

- relevance of the teaching to the personal situation of young people
- involvement with worship and prayer (the latter perhaps in groups), giving them both a sense of responsibility and a realisation of the task to be done, plus an acknowledgement that it can only be done with God's help
- encouragement to attend every week even if parents miss church.
- total focus on learning the Scriptures, as knowledge of the Bible is so disastrously poor, even among many churchgoing families. (A return to learning Bible memory verses?)
- help given to be able to answer criticisms like 'The Bible is out of date', 'Science has disproved religion' or 'Jesus was just a good man'

It is clear too that the teaching process has also radically changed, and that part of the need is to equip teachers not only with knowledge of how to teach, and the materials with which to teach, but also the confidence that, yes, perhaps, they *can* teach.

Within this context, the context of the Sunday School, the church is changing. The context of the church, society, is changing too. And the focus of the Sunday School, the child, is also changing, and to this we now turn.

Society and Young People

There is no doubt that young people in Britain today are under much greater pressure than their parents or grandparents were at similar ages – pressure essentially to conform to societal standards which are often at variance with traditional morality and traditional Christian teaching.

Sexual pressure

Although the legal age of consent may be sixteen, it is said that police rarely prosecute today when both perpetrators are under age. The number of teenage conceptions fell from 8.2% of women under twenty in 1971 to 5.9% in 1995.[1] In 1995:

0.1% of girls aged 14 or under conceived a baby
1.8% aged 15
4.0% aged 16
6.2% aged 17
8.1% aged 18, and
9.0% aged 19

This adds up to some 100,000 conceptions, many of which would have ended in abortion. Teenagers in the UK are more likely to become parents than anywhere else in Europe. Women who have early pregnancies tend to complete their education early, have poorer employment prospects, become dependent on welfare subsidies and report poorer health.

These statistics are but the thin end of the wedge, however. How many children lose their virginity in their teenage years, outside marriage, is not known definitively, but is thought to be perhaps as high as 75%. A survey of churched young people[2] in 1997 found that 12% of them had gone all the way, down from 18% in 1991. However, 27% had fondled genitals, 36% breasts and 59% had been involved in heavy 'French' kissing.

Whether this figure is even approximately correct or not, it illustrates the enormous sexual pressure that many young people face. Standing out as a Christian and saying no to pre-marital sex is thus extremely hard. One Christian fifteen-year-old told me a few months ago that there were a number of Christian girls in her school who saw nothing wrong in sleeping around. Will the lowering of the homosexual age of consent make matters worse?

A study in 1997 by Dr Roger Ingham, Reader in Psychology at Southampton University, found that children in homes that discuss sex stay virgins longer.[3] Another study in 1996 by Peter Vardy, author of *The Puzzle of Sex*, found that among A-level students (sixteen- to eighteen-year-olds), 85% of Roman Catholics and 80% of Anglicans did not think it was morally wrong to have sex with a long-term partner when not married, and 63% and 60% respectively did not think sex between male homosexuals to be 'always' morally wrong.[4] On the other hand, 87% of young people 'do not feel at ease in the company of gays and lesbians'.[5]

A senior minister of a well-known Baptist Church was addressing a conference of ministers. 'When did you last marry a virgin?' he asked of them. There was silence.

Drug pressure

The *British Crime Survey* undertaken by the Home Office in 1996 revealed that of those aged sixteen to nineteen:

35% had tried cannabis
16% amphetamines
10% LSD
 9% Ecstasy
 7% magic mushroom
 5% solvents
 4% cocaine, crack or heroin

Almost half, 45%, had tried at least one of these, which means that on average most sixteen- to nineteen-year olds had tried two in the above list. The use of illicit drugs has increased since the 1970s, mostly among the older teens and those in their early 20s.[6]

Christian young people are not immune to such temptations. What is the best way to produce teaching material in the context of a Sunday School, Youth or Holiday Club programme to warn them of the dangers? A survey of young people attending Spring Harvest in 1995[7] found that 23% of those aged twelve to sixteen had been offered drugs and 10% had tried them, and 47% of those seventeen or over had been offered them and 23% had tried them.

Another 1997 survey[8] found that 19% of churchgoing pupils aged fifteen and sixteen with a high Christian commitment, 33% with a medium commitment and 55% with a low commitment agreed with the statement that 'It's all right to use soft drugs like marijuana'. Attitudes to drug use also varied by denomination, as shown in Table 8:

Table 8: Percentage of churchgoing pupils disapproving the use of various substances, 1997

Denomination	Alcohol	Tobacco	Marijuana	Butane	Heroin	Glue
	%	%	%	%	%	%
Roman Catholic	19	42	54	72	75	76
Anglican	20	42	56	75	80	80
Mainstream Protestant	30	50	63	75	81	84
Other Protestant	46	68	74	83	87	85

Crime pressure

Almost two-fifths of offenders cautioned or convicted for indictable offences in 1996 were under twenty-one. A third (34%) of men and 9% of women born in 1958 had had a conviction for a standard list offence by the age of thirty-four! A small proportion of offenders are responsible for a large proportion of offences, as, for example, 7% of men born in 1958 had appeared in court four or more times by the time they were thirty, accounting for 23% of offenders but 60% of crimes.[9]

Figure 13: Criminal offenders by gender and age, 1996, as a percentage of the population

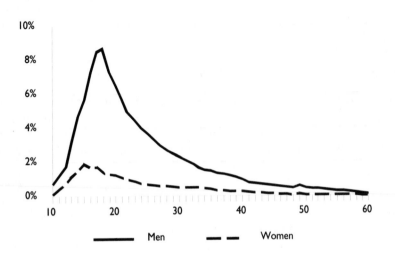

Again, Christian young people are not immune from these kinds of temptation either. How do we teach them not to be involved in petty (or serious) crime? This is made more difficult when adult Christians' standards towards other people's property is made explicit.

In the *Ansvar Survey of English Social Behaviour*,[10] respondents were asked how acceptable they found various actions. Not paying your fares on public transport, not declaring all your income (so paying less income tax), keeping extra change when given you by mistake, taking sick leave when you were well, claiming more expenses than you were entitled to, were all deemed inappropriate by Christian people – though much less so by non-Christians.

However, taking home an office Biro for your own use, saying the boss was out when s/he was in, making personal use of the firm's photocopier without paying for it, making private use of the office phone, again without payment, were all deemed acceptable by Christian people, and even more so by non-Christians.

Suicide

Suicide among men aged fifteen to twenty-four jumped from one per 10,000 in the 1970s to 1.5 in the 1980s, and to 1.8 in the early 1990s, though it has since fallen back to 1.5. The women's rate has consistently been about one per 20,000 throughout this period. In 1992, suicides accounted for 12% of all deaths for men aged fifteen to nineteen, and 25% for men aged twenty to twenty-four. What proportion of these are Christians is not known, but almost certainly some are. Is this a further issue that needs attention in teaching materials? The well-publicised deaths of those known to be Christian, like the former SAS officer who killed himself, do not help young people wondering how they can cope. The numbers who take their life because of examination pressure either at school or university again publicise this way of being unable to cope.

Trends in marriage and divorce

Mark Twain may have been right! 'Love seems the swiftest,' he said, 'but it is the slowest of all growths. No man or woman really knows what perfect love is until they have been married a quarter of a century.'[11] But, from all the statistics of divorces, one might assume that hardly any ever celebrate their silver anniversary. Not true!

In 1993, 51% of men and 49% of women in the population were both married (showing marriage is popular), and in their first marriage (showing divorce is not quite as prevalent as often suggested).[12] Almost half of marriages (47%) reach their silver anniversary, and a further 14% would have done so had not one partner died first. Six per cent of couples celebrate their golden anniversary, and a further 53% would if death did not intervene.

This is not to suggest that divorce does not happen, but simply to put divorce into its context of a very large number of first marriages (over thirteen million) in Britain today. There are a further two million couples in their second or subsequent marriage. Between 1971 and 1995 the number of marriages and re-marriages each year declined, however, from 460,000 to 320,000 and the number of divorces increased from 80,000 to 170,000. The number of divorces has remained roughly constant since the mid-1980s, whereas the number of marriages has declined steadily, as Figure 14 illustrates.

Figure 14: Marriages and divorces 1971-1995, UK

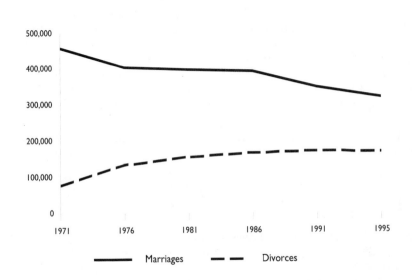

Relating the annual number of divorces to the number of marriages, it can appear that half of all marriages end in divorce, but this ignores the thirteen million marriages, most of which will not end in divorce. It is, however, true that the likelihood of divorce is higher today than in the mid-1970s. It is now reckoned that two in five marriages will fail.[13]

In 1995, four weddings in nine (44%) were in a church, including 60% of people marrying for the first time. The number is decreasing, however, as civil weddings can now be held in other approved premises apart from a registry office. Eighty-five per cent of women marrying in an Anglican church in 1993 were in their twenties, as were 81% of those marrying in a Roman Catholic church, but only 59% of those marrying in a Methodist church. The latter denomination allows more divorced people to marry in church and they tend to be older.[14]

The long-term decline of marriage is likely to continue. The Government Actuary predicts that married people will, for the first time since 1801 when census records began, become a minority: 48% of the population by 2011, and 45% by 2020.[15] It is not the increase in cohabiting which accounts for the decrease, but people living alone. Half of all men now aged between thirty and forty-four will remain single up to 2021, and more than half will be living on their own by 2016.

Despite all this, the popularity of the marriage concept is still high: 69% of those surveyed in a MORI poll still believe that to be 'married with children' is the most desirable way to live,[16] and it is this ideal that needs to be upheld.

Should Christian organisations continue to emphasise the importance of marriage based on the biblical principle (and urge the government to reverse some of its tax policies), or should it concentrate instead on the importance of parenthood and what this means? Alan Storkey in his book, *Marriage and its Modern Crisis*,[17] rightly highlights the final word in its title. 'Features of contemporary marriage make it unprecedentedly unstable: changes in the philosophy of marriage, the problem of power in gender relationships, the sexualisation of society, changes in marriage law, and the effects of new work patterns.' Do we do better then to avoid 'marriage' and concentrate instead on 'family'? From a child's point of view, love, care, mutual support and respect are the key characteristics that for them define 'family'.[18]

A 1990 Council of Europe conference on the population of Europe forecast that the pattern of family life in Scandinavia would become the norm for Europe over the subsequent twenty years. That could mean as many as 70% of children born out of wedlock, and an increase in homosexual marriages, legalised in Denmark in 1993, with their first homosexual divorce a year later.

If there is pressure to recognise cohabitation as legally equivalent to marriage, without its permanent commitment and responsibilities, there will appear even less reason to get married. Such recognition would in addition mean putting same-sex unions on a par with marriage.[19]

The impact of divorce

The large number of marriages means that teaching materials must continue to emphasise the importance of family. However, the frequency of divorce means that Sunday School and youth materials cannot overlook this aspect of life.

One woman in ten in her thirties and forties in Britain in 1994 had been divorced; the figure was slightly lower for men. In 1995 there were 161,000 children in families which had gone through divorce. About a quarter of today's children can expect their parents to divorce before they are sixteen, or before they take their GCSE exams.

There is little evidence on the number of Christian divorces, but such as there is (from an examination of census details in Northern Ireland in 1991[20]) suggests that Christians divorce at half the rate of non-Christians.

This still means that one child in eight in a Christian home will experience their parents' divorce. In a Sunday School of fifty children aged three to ten, five on average will experience divorce while at that Sunday School.

How should children cope? How can they be helped to understand that it is not their fault (many children believe that somehow they have contributed to the break-up)? How can we help children to understand priorities when Sunday is 'Daddy's day'? Or help them to understand God as 'Father' when they may have no father-figure in their lives? Teaching materials must somehow deal with these questions.

Research has shown that children from a broken home are more likely to:

- become parents at an early age
- divorce if they marry
- suffer a break-up if they cohabit
- have illegitimate children
- have few qualifications
- have low status employment or be unemployed
- live in council accommodation or be homeless
- be involved in crime

This is a horrendous list![21]

Figure 15: Children in divorcing families, 1971-95[22]

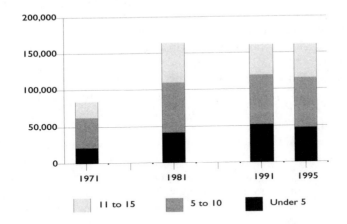

Divorce also hits men in many instances, who 'disengage' from family life. Divorce also means more homes will be required.

The popularity of cohabitation

'Cohabitation' means a man and a woman living together without being married. There are 1.5 million cohabiting couples, comprising 7% of all adults over sixteen years of age (up from 4% in 1989). This is likely to rise to three million by 2021.[23] By age group these are:

Table 9: Percentage cohabiting by age group, 1993

Age	Men (%)	Women (%)
16-24	8	12
25-34	14	11
35-44	6	5
Over 44	7	5
All ages	7	7

Many of these couples subsequently get married (usually within two years, unless a family is started earlier).

What percentage of couples marrying in church had cohabited first (based on couples giving the same address when registering[24])? An article in *Population Trends*,[25] gave a figure of 41%, but it was suggested this could be an under-estimate of up to 20%. This suggests that least three couples in five marrying in church cohabit first!

This figure of 41% is, however, an average, calculated from varying denominations/religions: the Religious Society of Friends was 70%, United Reformed Church 65%, Methodists 62%, Roman Catholics 48%, Baptists 41%, Salvation Army 40%, Muslims 39%, Church of England 36%, Jews 34%, Church in Wales 23%, Christian Brethren 20%, with 7% each for Jehovah's Witnesses and Sikhs.

The sheer number of cohabiting couples – 1.5 million – means that this feature of societal life cannot be ignored either. However, as many cohabiting couples do not have children, the impact on Sunday School is likely to be less than the numbers might suggest. There will, however, be some children in our Sunday Schools whose parents are not married, and the teaching materials need to be written so that these children do not feel disadvantaged because their parents haven't 'tied the knot'.

The problem is not the numbers who cohabit as such, but that it is seen as an acceptable lifestyle. Recent research by Barnardos showed that 82% of girls and 78% of boys agreed with the statement, 'It is all right for a couple to live together without intending to get married'.[26] It is thus important not only to stress a biblical view of marriage, but also to be able to help those who believe this to have the courage to maintain it in the face of almost overwhelming numbers denying it.

Commitment

What does this mean for commitment? Only 14% of girls and 22% of boys agree that 'where there are children in the family, parents should stay together even if they don't get along'.[27] If commitment to the most intimate union known to human beings is repeatedly thrown asunder, what of other commitments?

On a much lesser scale, commitment to church membership has declined, as it has to many other organisations – apparently a characteristic of today's society. What, then, of commitment to even deeper things than organisations or people – to Christ? Will there be a tendency for those who are Christians in their twenties today, for example, to say in their forties, 'Well, I've followed Christianity for the last twenty years, now I'll try Buddhism.'?

The biblical basis of commitment, or perseverance, is very strong. 'The one who endures to the end will be saved'[28] is but one text of many. In our dealings with young people today, how do we help to encourage their commitment to spiritual values and beliefs? Commitment is partly built up around action. Do we need to teach again the importance of a daily act of devotion, and the expression of one's faith in certain mores?

This issue was highlighted by evidence given to the Parliamentary Hearing on the Family in the United Nations Year of the Family in 1994. Dr Kiernan, Senior Research Fellow in Demography at the London School of Economics, argued that the main engine driving the change in couples living together is that of *partnership* behaviour. Partnerships were not relationships, and were of a different quality. Marriage is now seen as such an alliance, a relationship, not a partnership. Hence the need to teach about relationships in terms of acceptance, tolerance, expectations and communications. Cohabitation is another form of relationship, not a partnership. A partnership often begins when a couple has a baby, or at least is perceived as needing to begin: 70% in 1989 accepted the statement that 'people who want children ought to get married'.[29]

The Cambridge-based Relationships Foundation started by Dr Michael Schluter has identified a further category of those who are disadvantaged: 'the relationally deprived.'[30] Nigel Lee, Head of Student Ministries at the Universities and Colleges Christian Fellowship, told a meeting at which I was present[31] of how there is 'less and less communal space in new student accommodation'. There was a diminution of mature social conversation. The consequence was a lack of understanding of relationships with anybody (let alone Jesus Christ), and hence a need for teaching on this topic.

This becomes especially important when teenagers want to talk things over with their parents. Fitting in these times of precious conversation (invariably in my experience at the most inconvenient and pressurised times of the day!) becomes a priority. Andy Hickford, formerly a youth pastor in Luton, says, 'we soon discovered that a teenager's world revolved around school and family'.[32] Another church leader said, 'The problems of growing up in a divorced or remarried home makes teenagers more realistic of the need of something beyond themselves to help themselves, especially women.'

Lone parenthood

Twenty-two per cent of all families in 1996 were headed by a lone parent, all bar 2% lone mothers. About 4% of these are families where the parent is a widow or widower; a third, 34%, are lone single mothers. (Full details are in Table 10.) 'In just one generation the number of first-time marriages has halved, the number of divorces trebled and the population of children born outside of marriage quadrupled.'[33] It is often the children in this last category that live in single parent homes.

There are the obvious theological difficulties in referring to 'God the Father' when a child may have no experience of a father. But it is in the sociological impact that this deprivation is likely to be felt most – and a few, maybe not Christian, would say it was no deprivation!

If many lone parent families are headed by mothers, will this begin to form a more matriarchal society? If fathers tend to opt out of family involvement because of divorce, feel the loss of status because of unemployment, and have increasingly to compete with women for scarce jobs, what does this mean for society and for the young people in it? In the UK there are currently 2,500,000 children in lone-mother families, 75% of whom rarely if ever see their fathers.[34] The media emphasise this change, perhaps unconsciously. *Men Behaving Badly* portrays men as 'lager-swilling feckless louts' and the women as 'smart and clever'.[35] Girls out-perform boys in most areas of education. In their heyday, the Spice Girls epitomised 'girl power'. Television generates a culture which is feminist, humourless and non/anti-Christian. The seemingly relentless march to matriarchy becomes yet another trend to be put into biblical perspective.

Population changes

Irrespective of the pressures on young people, and the kind of family in which they may be brought up, how many of them are there? There were 10.8 million children under fifteen in 1986 in the UK, which will rise to 11.8 million by 2001, and fall back again to 11 million by 2011. Trends in the number of children, and the population of working age, reflect previous birth patterns. The main points of importance at the beginning of the twenty-first century are:

- There are rather more people aged between 36 and 54, because of the post-Second World War births' peak and the consequential second-generation mid-1960s' baby boom.
- The number of people of working age is likely to increase until 2011

when it will then fall as the boomers of the 1960s begin to retire.

- Women have entered the working population in large numbers.
- There are fewer people than might be expected aged between 24 and 35, because of the paucity of births in the early 1950s and the very small number in 1977 (one of the few years when deaths exceeded births).
- From age 9 to 23 the numbers rise above expectations, from the births' trough in 1977 to a peak in 1990, because of the third-generation echo of the post-war 'bulge'.
- There are fewer aged under 9 pro rata, which is projected to continue until 2007.[36]

What are the implications of these changes?[37] These turning-points in the population will move up through the age range as time passes, so that, for instance:

- The numbers at the usual age of entry for higher education will rise for the next ten years. How far these will be affected long term by the present government's decision to charge students for tuition remains to be seen.
- On the other hand, the numbers entering primary school, currently falling, will continue to decline for some time. As church Sunday Schools reflect numbers in the population, this means there will be fewer in the Sunday School simply because there are fewer children in the target age group.
- The so-called 'dependency ratio' of working population to non-working will remain fairly constant up to 2011 but could then increase, depending on the economic activity of those then retiring. Those in their sixties now interact more with their community and spend more than those retiring twenty years or so ago.
- The size of families has fallen – from an average of 2.45 children in the 1930s to an estimated 1.80 for women born after 1975, 14% less than the 2.1 required to replace the population (immigration apart), if mortality rates were constant. This is due to a number of factors, including more women now working, increased affluence and better contraception.
- The proportion of women who will never have a child is rising. For women born in the 'boomer' years of the 1960s, this proportion is currently about one in ten, although there are still a few years to go before their childbearing years are over. But the signs are that this proportion has risen, and is continuing to rise, and could reach a level of one in four or five women. This means therefore fewer parents, and if parents are the most likely to be willing to be Sunday School teachers (because after all they have first-hand experience of looking after children), then the number of potential teachers is falling and likely to continue to fall. Of course, there are many either

single women or childless married women who also help in Sunday School, but will they continue to come forward in such numbers as they have? Are such people actually present in our churches in the same proportions as in the population? This is simply not known.

- Women are also starting their families later, obviously another contributing factor to smaller families, mainly because they are marrying later. This means that parents are older today than they were – and possibly therefore have less energy. Also, if both partners are working, they do not want to have commitments on their day off (Sunday).
- The steep rise in children born outside marriage has already been noted. The proportion of single or unmarried parents who are in church is smaller than population proportions in every survey we have done where this has been measured. It is partly of course because churches by and large do not welcome those whose lifestyle is judged 'inappropriate' or just plain 'wrong' if you are Christian. So about a third of children are unlikely even to be considered for Sunday School, again making the numbers attending overall sharply down.
- Remarriage has also been briefly mentioned, but 9% of men and 6% of women are in their second or third (or subsequent) marriage. Many of these two million households will include children and step-children. In many, the marital experience of the parents will again be judged (by them, the parents) 'unsuitable' for their participation in church, and the children/step-children in their household again less likely to attend Sunday School. Hence a further reduction in overall numbers.

There is a further population change, mainly affecting Western countries, which is taking place over a much longer time scale.[38] A study in the *British Medical Journal* in 1992 summarised sixty-one research projects involving 15,000 men with no history of infertility. The average sperm count in 1940 was 113 million per millilitre; by 1990, it had fallen to 66 million. There was also a fall in the motility, or healthiness, of the sperm. If this trend continues, it means that millions of men will be unable to father children over the next fifty years.

Family composition

The pattern of family life has been changing during the 1990s and is likely to continue to do so. Table 10[39] takes figures from the *General Household Survey* (GHS) historically, but the projection for 2000, a linear progression, is personal. The boxes in the first row in this table are totals of the subsequent boxes. Thus in 1990, for example, the married couple family figure of 76% in the first row is the total of 22% married couples in 'Couple Families with no children', 43% 'Couple families with dependent children' and 11% 'Couple familes with only non-dependent children'. Likewise for cohabiting couples and lone parent families.

Table 10: Family composition in Great Britain, 1986-2000

Type of family with head aged under 60	1986 %	1988 %	1990 %	1992 %	1994 %	2000 %
Married-couple families:[1]	82	79	76	74	71	62
Cohabiting-couple families[1]	5	8	8	9	11	15
Lone-parent families[2]	13	13	16	16	18	23
Couple families with no children:						
Married couples	22	22	22	21	21	20
Cohabiting couples	3	5	5	6	7	10
Couple families with dependent children:						
Married couples	49	46	43	42	42	35
Cohabiting couples	2	3	3	3	4	5
Couple families with only non-dependent children:						
Married couples	11	11	11	11	8	7
Cohabiting couples	0.3	0.3	0.4	0.3	0.2	0.2
Lone parent families with dependent children:						
Lone single mothers	2	3	4	5	5	8
Lone separated mothers	2	2	2	3	3	4
Lone divorced mothers	4	4	4	4	5	6
Lone widowed mothers	0.5	0.6	0.6	0.5	0.6	0.6
Lone fathers	0.8	0.8	0.8	1	1	1
Lone parent families with only non-dependent children:	3	3	4	3	3	3
All families[1]: Sample size (=100%)	5,003	4,974	4,740	4,899	4,621	n/a

[1] With or without children

[2] With either dependent children, non-dependent children, or both

This table shows very clearly the tripling of cohabiting couples and the doubling of lone parent families in the population in fifteen years. The importance of these figures is simply that the proportions of these types of families who attend church is small, although there has been no study which actually measures this. One large study for a major Christian agency showed that the proportion of supporters who were divorced or separated had increased from 1% in 1991 to 3% in 1995. While this means a larger number of such people were willing to help that agency, support of a Christian agency does not necessarily correspond with church attendance. In any case, such a small increase when the population increase is much larger supports the suggestion that churches by and large do not welcome dysfunctional families.

Table 10 also supports the previous comment that cohabiting couples whilst cohabiting are less likely to have children than married couples. The real change is between 'traditional' families with children and lone-parent families, and in the latter the major change is with single mothers rather than divorced or separated mothers. Even if a church accepts divorced or separated mothers, it is perhaps less likely to welcome single mothers. Hence there are fewer women of child-bearing age in church.

This has two consequences. There are fewer teachers to teach in Sunday School, and thus the high proportion of older teachers (26% in their fifties, 15% in their sixties in one large study) is likely to continue. It also means that when single parents *do* come to church, they are much more likely to want to be in church rather than in the Sunday School.

This suggests the importance of encouraging older parents and grandparents to keep on teaching, and helping them to be equipped to do so, faced with modern young people. Does it mean moving 'Sunday' School to other days, or evenings, because children are more available then? The Salvation Army in Bromley, Kent, now have Monday School not Sunday School. Could this become a pattern for the future? Does it have significance that such moves will take place invariably in the evenings rather than the mornings, and is the attendance time of such meetings longer or shorter than the church service/sermon slot?

Types of household

There is one further related change that needs to be mentioned – the composition of households, which is not the same as composition of families. These are given in Table 11[40] (figures for 2000 are a personal estimate).

Table 11: Household composition, Great Britain, 1961–2000

Type of household	1961 %	1971 %	1981 %	1991 %	1994 %	2000 %
One-person households	12	18	22	27	27	30
Married couple households	74	70	65	59	58	55
Lone-parent households	6	7	9	10	11	12
Other types of household	8	5	4	4	4	3
One-person households:						
Under pensionable age	4	6	8	11	12	13
Over pensionable age	8	12	14	16	15	17
Married couple households with:						
No children	26	27	26	26	27	27
1-2 dependent children[1]	30	26	25	20	20	18
3+ dependent children[1]	8	9	6	5	5	4
Non-dependent children only	10	8	8	8	6	6
Lone parent households with:						
Dependent children[1]	2	3	5	6	7	8
Non-dependent children only	4	4	4	4	4	4
Other types of household:						
Two or more unrelated adults	5	4	3	3	3	2
Two or more families	3	1	1	1	1	1
Number of households[2] (=100%)	16.2	18.2	19.5	22.4	23.1	24.1

[1] May also include some non-dependent children

[2] In millions

The number of one-person households with the occupant under pensionable age is increasing, from 4% in 1961 to an anticipated 13% in 2000. Should teaching materials help prepare children for bachelorhood and spinsterhood?

Table 11 also shows the decreasing size in families, which inevitably means fewer children in church. To maintain the same number of children overall, the church has to compensate by reaching more families, more households, more units.

(There is some disparity between the numbers in certain groups in Tables 10 and 11. This is because the source is different. Table 10 comes from a sample survey, the *General Household Survey*, which means that the percentages are less reliable. Table 11 comes from the population censuses which are as accurate as one is going to get, though the figures for 1994 in Table 11 are from the GHS also.)

So what does all this mean?

It means that:

- The structure of society is changing, with permanence and stability no longer key characteristics.
- Family life as we know it is fast declining and it will not be long before a majority of people in the UK choose to live another way. This way will tend to be the choice of the unchurched rather than the churched, although there will always be exceptions. It means therefore that we are entering a period where cross-cultural mission evangelism principles become of major importance.
- Christian agencies have to think through the implications of dysfunctional families and what that means for children, parents and teachers.
- Children today are brought up in a sex-obsessed culture where they often learn the facts of life by experience rather than in the context of moral and/or Christian teaching. The implications of sleeping together will be visible to them everywhere – at home, at school, via the media, among neighbours and friends. They cannot escape the incessant demands to conform to their peers.
- Nothing is certain – except that nothing is certain! No one knows when change will occur. 'Thank goodness,' said the child of our next-door neighbours when told her parents were divorcing, 'now we are like the rest in our class.'
- Numbers are decreasing: population numbers in total, and numbers in church. In churches, there is also a decline in respect of frequency of attendance, and also willingness to be actively involved.
- Commitment is in rare supply. It is well on the way to becoming an unknown word, just as relationship can so easily be the new spelling of partnership. How do we encourage and teach the currently untrendy attributes such as endurance? When the Son of Man returns, will he find faith on the earth?[41]

Key Factors
of Church Life

There are obviously many other facets of church life apart from the concern for young people and work among them. We have already looked at church people generally, and church leaders. This chapter in some ways summarises the previous ones and focuses more on what might be thought of as aspects of church programme.

Some key statistics of church life at the moment are:

- 63% of the population profess to be Christian, a proportion which is slowly decreasing, while the proportion belonging to other faiths is rising.[1]
- 11% of the population belong to a church as a church member. The Church of England, Church of Scotland and Roman Catholics (with Mass attendance used in lieu of membership) account for 69% of the total, which shows that the other 200+ denominations are on average very small. The largest are the Methodists, Baptists, Pentecostals and New Churches.
- 8% of the population go to church on any given Sunday, but the following Sunday it is not the same 8%! *The English Church Attendance Survey* showed that 7.5% went each week in England in 1998 but 10.2% once a month.

In the decade 1990 to 2000 the church in the UK lost 750,000 members, or an average of 75,000 a year. This is the difference between 275,000 joining and 350,000 leaving per year. Of the joiners:

- 45% moved from one church to another, mostly because they moved house, so these were not new members.
- 26% who joined were children in church reaching the age to become members in their own right. These were new members but not new attenders.
- 11% were ex-members coming back to church.
- 18% were converts,[2] or 50,000 people a year, one per church on average.[3]

Of the 350,000 members who left:

- 22% died
- 36% moved and rejoined another church
- 20% moved, didn't rejoin another church but just attended instead
- 13% left the church disillusioned and did not return, and
- 9% left the church disillusioned and will return, on average in about eight years' time [4]

A similar analysis of attenders rather than members revealed that in the decade 1990 to 2000, a net 580,000 stopped going to church: 58,000 a year, made up of 139,000 who stopped and 81,000 who started. Of the latter:

- 50,000 were conversions
- 31,000 returned to churchgoing having been away

Of the 139,000 who stopped attending:

- 31,000 left but will eventually return
- 45,000 left not to return
- 58,000 started attending once a fortnight (equivalent to 29,000 a week stopping)
- 34,000 died

If the detail of these numbers confuses, look at the broad overview: in the past twenty years, 1.6 million people (about 2.5% of the population) have started going to church. Over the same time we have lost 2.8 million, a quarter through death, and three-quarters for other, perhaps preventable, reasons. We are simply losing more people than we gain, and the rate of loss is accelerating (although this is not apparent in the above figures).

These are sad numbers. They show the importance of encouraging regular church attendance, and the need to try and ensure existing attenders don't stop. *Keeping* people is as important in church life as *reaching* people. What then are some of the factors which cause people to stay or go?

Leaving church

Two pieces of research, both published in 1993, looked at why people left church. Michael Fanstone,[5] minister of Emmanuel Baptist Church, Gravesend, Kent, interviewed over 500 people who no longer regularly attended church and found that (some giving more than one reason):

- 62% had left because they felt that church was no longer relevant
- 44% for a variety of personal reasons
- 27% because of the minister or the way the church was going
- 7% because of 'God issues' – crises of faith such as sudden illness, disaster, or death with which a person's faith was unable to cope

Eddie Gibbs' international study agreed with these findings, but added one more – the fact that some leave because they are asked to do too much in a church.[6] A significant study by Dr Gavin Wakefield, then a team vicar in Essex, looked at the reasons people give for moving and joining churches.[7] When people move house (and committed churchgoers appear to do so less than the general population), they generally choose the nearest church (50%), though style of worship is also important (32%). He explores in some depth whether people change denomination when they move house. Only 27% did so. On the other hand, almost exactly double that proportion, 53%, changed denomination without moving house. Anglicans were less likely to change denomination.

However, when people leave a church they dislike, 54% look for a church whose worship they like, and 37% for preaching they enjoy. Preaching is a key element in church life, especially in drawing newcomers.

A further study of people leaving church[8] showed that 92% said that no one had talked to them about why their attendance at church had been dropping. The research suggested there was on average about a six-week 'cooling-off' period. Even so, 45% who left kept open the possibility of returning at a later time.

Preaching

The average sermon was apparently thirty minutes long at the beginning of the twentieth century, but only seven minutes at its end. What do people, especially irregular or non-churchgoers, want when they go to church? An Australian study found that 76% wanted 'a short, simple sermon'.[9] Surveys by the Baptist Union of Ireland[10] have found that sermons are much less likely to be 'always helpful', as Figure 16 below shows. The key age is sixteen- and seventeen-year-olds, whose reactions to sermons are about average – younger people are more likely to be switched off by them, older people less so. Perhaps that is the target age preachers should aim for.

Figure 16: 'Do you find the Sunday Sermon helpful?'

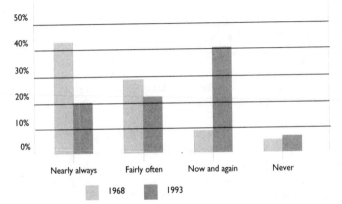

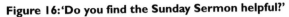

Young people who frequently complain that church is 'boring' often mean that they find the sermons too long,[11] or too uninteresting. This is not just true of young people, however. In a survey in 1997, Mark Greene, then Vice Principal (Community) of London Bible College, found it was true of older people also. On a helpfulness scale of 0–4, he found that sermons were helpful in:

2.6 personal areas
2.1 church areas
1.8 home areas
1.7 work areas

He concluded, 'The reality seems to be that the further a Christian gets from the church building, the less likely they are to have an adequate base of teaching to lead their lives in a godly manner.'[12] He summarised: 'many ministers are actually out of touch with their people', and suggested they find out whether their sermons helped people. They also needed to know what people do. Could ministers answer the question: 'It's eleven o'clock on Monday: where are your people and what issues and opportunities do they have right now?'

As we face church for the future, the issue of the Sunday sermon cannot be ignored.

Women

Women have been in ministry for years! William Booth was one of the more enlightened men in the nineteenth century when he allowed women to serve as full Salvation Army officers. They have served with distinction in the overseas missionary movement and, since 1994, have been allowed to be ordained in the Church of England, one of the most important bastions on the path to collegiate acceptance.[13] Some 8% of the ministers in Britain are female, with some denominations (of which the Roman Catholics are the largest) having none, and others (like the Church of Scotland and United Reformed Church) with high percentages.

Much of the focus on women has been in this leadership capacity, but women have served in many other roles as well, of which helping with young people in the Sunday School or elsewhere is very common. In fact, without women the Sunday School movement would long ago have packed up!

But there is another element in this, not of leadership or service, but simply women in church. A detailed survey on women and the church[14] showed that women primarily come to church because of relationships – they will meet their friends, find out what has happened to so-and-so, be able to talk to this person, or have a cup of tea with that person, and arrange to visit this person who has been ill, or make a cake,[15] etc. This is not just a social outworking. A survey found that in churches where the majority of people had their closest friends, they were much more likely to have felt they had grown spiritually in the previous year.

These few paragraphs are not meant to pre-empt what will be shown in the book to be published on this research, but simply to act as a marker that this is an extremely important issue.

Prayer

Many would say that the prayer life of the church is vital. So is the prayer life of the individual. But not much research has been undertaken to find out who prays, how much people pray, when they pray, their experience in prayer, or what they pray for.

A survey of Anglican ministers in the 1970s apparently found they prayed for an average of eight minutes a day. Peter Wagner, who has written many books on prayer, suggests Christians should pray personally for at least twenty minutes a day, but admits that he himself doesn't do this. This was based on a survey of American pastors whose average time of prayer was 22 minutes daily. He also found by way of comparison that:

- Australian pastors prayed for an average of 23 minutes daily
- New Zealand pastors - an average of 30 minutes daily
- Japanese pastors - 44 minutes daily
- Korean pastors - an average of 90 minutes daily[16]

Another American study of 1,700 Wesleyan churches found that their ministers prayed for an average of twenty-five minutes a day. The amount they prayed seemed to make no difference as to whether their church grew or not, but there were significant differences between ministers who prayed weekly with a prayer group and those who didn't. The former were more likely to have a growing church (59% to 51%).[17]

A survey of both church members and non-members in 1986 in Scotland found that 60% of Roman Catholics prayed every day, 44% of Christians in smaller denominations, 36% of those in the Church of Scotland, and 19% of those outside the church![18]

Students at Sheffield University were surveyed by Dr John Mulholland[19] over twenty-four years. In 1961, 65% said private prayers, 31% daily. In 1972 these percentages were 42% and 16% respectively, and in 1985 they were 30% and 9%, a clear decrease in private praying by students, by half in numbers praying, and by a third in frequency.

Secondary school pupils have been regularly surveyed by Leslie Francis, formerly the D J James Professor of Pastoral Theology at Trinity College, Carmarthen. One of his questions asks if they 'believe that God listens to my prayers'. In 1974, 47% said they did, a percentage which had fallen to 29% by 1986 but rose to 31% by 1994.[20] A 1997 survey among church youth by Christian Research for Agapé[21] found that 45% of eleven- to thirteen-year-olds prayed daily, a percentage which rose to 70%

for those aged eighteen or nineteen.

Of a sample of 1,500 people in an American survey[22] in the early 1990s:

- 70% experienced a deep sense of peace and well-being when they prayed
- 59% felt the strong presence of God
- 47% received a definite answer to a specific request
- 40% received a deeper insight into spiritual/biblical truth
- 37% felt divinely inspired or 'led by God' to perform a specific action regularly or occasionally

What do people pray for? Another American study[23] indicated that:

- 82% pray for health or success for a child or family member
- 75% pray for strength to overcome a personal weakness
- 73% say prayers for help in finding a job
- 36% never prayed for financial or career success

At least these are better than one person surveyed in this country who, when asked what he prayed for, replied that his horses would win! Another non-believer asked her Christian sister to pray she would win the National Lottery!

This summary does not show a vast amount of research on the topic of prayer, and what there is suggests a decline in the practice of prayer, especially by young people and students. But even those outside the church pray, sometimes regularly. Those inside perhaps pray more; certainly leadership example is important. There are tangible benefits from prayer, even if much of it is self- or family-centred.

One of the largest surveys on prayer in the UK was conducted by the Teal Trust in 1998.[24] It was estimated to represent one in eight churchgoers. Approximately a third of respondents (35%) spent an hour or more in personal prayer each week, with obviously two-thirds spending less. An hour a week is equivalent to nine minutes a day. What did they pray about? The top items were:

- family and friends (89%)
- things to thank God for (80%)
- health/healing of particular people (67%)
- praising and worshipping God (65%)
- confessing things to God (58%)

The work of the church came next with 44%, then asking that specific people would come to faith (33%). The biggest barrier to prayer was wandering thoughts, with 80% finding this at least sometimes a problem. Noise was a distraction for two-thirds, and just over half, 54%, 'struggle to find time'. Although 84% felt it was important that Christians should pray together as well as alone, only 39% actually did so outside church services. The survey found that only a quarter of Christian couples pray together either every day or most days.

What did people experience as a result of praying? These are given in Table 12 below, and show that answered prayer is high in their belief:

Table 12: Experiences in prayer by time spent praying

Percentage of respondents who ...	Time spent praying per week		Overall
	Under 1 hour	Over 1 hour	
Believe God hears their prayers	90	98	93
Believe they have experienced answered prayer	81	96	86
Spend time listening to God	54	80	63
Have experienced God communicating with them while they pray	49	77	59
Read the Bible every day or most days	44	82	58
Pray with others at least once a week	31	52	39

However, the more interesting aspects of Table 12 are the differences between those who pray less than, and more than, an hour a week. The differences in the last four categories of prayer experience are wide and significant. Listening and talking with God is much more likely with those who spend longer in prayer, and these also are more likely to be regular Bible readers and willing to pray with others. The length of time a person spends in prayer could be a crucial discriminator.

Prayer was one of the reasons Billy Graham gave for the success of his Wembley Crusade in 1954.[25] The evangelist Morris Cerullo believes that an 'energizing, global call to prayer is coming upon the people of God. As a result ... we will see the end gathering of the greatest harvest that this world has ever known!'[26]

Some, like UK evangelist Roger Carswell, 'have a long list of children for whom they pray' in their personal prayer diary.[27] Others encourage children to pray publicly. The International Global Consultation on World Evangelisation in Seoul, Korea, in 1995 had a small number of children among those who prayed every day for the event. 'There is a growing prayer movement, as represented by the Children's Global Prayer Movement, and the National Children's Prayer Network, where youngsters pray not only for their own needs but for such goals as world evangelism and national law-makers.'[28]

Prophecy

One of the issues on which the church is not united today is the role of biblical prophecy. Of the five aspects with which the management guru, John Adair, describes the church[29] (theological, historical, sociological, political and creative), it is the creative which he links with prophecy, and innovation, and imagination, and the future. He asks the question, 'What will the church be like in ten years' time?' and sees the answer to this as an extrapolation of the present, what he calls the 'think-tank' approach. His second question is, 'What ought the church to be like in ten years' time?' and this cannot be answered in the same way. It requires the principles of Horizon Mission Methodology described in the final chapter.

In order to pursue current issues on prophecy further, I visited three leaders in the New Churches and an evangelical Anglican minister of a large south London church. The differences between them are real. While the New Churches affirm the five-fold roles within the church of apostles, prophets, evangelists, pastors and teachers,[30] the first two of those roles are largely considered by others to have died out at the end of the apostolic era. Why? Well, at least with respect to the prophets because the biblical prophetic witness is largely 'soteriological', meaning that it relates to the first and second comings of the Lord Jesus Christ, and is essentially redemptive. Others in the New Churches totally disagree, and point to New Testament prophets such as Agabus.

The issue is important because of the key prophecy that many New Churches make in a variety of forms – that of some kind of coming revival. The value of these prophecies of revival is dependent on a whole range of 'lesser' prophecies. There is no doubt that some of these have been remarkable. In May 1997, Ginny Burgin, a Sheffield mother of two, received a very clear prophecy:

> 'I am at work in the heart and spirit of the people of this nation. I am doing a work which at the moment is very, very unseen. But it is happening quicker than you think. Things are happening much more quickly than you think. And as a sign – this shall be a sign – that there will be a day very soon when the whole nation will mourn: and the whole nation will put flowers in their cities.'[31]

It seemed very obviously fulfilled in the week after the tragic death of Diana, Princess of Wales, the first week of September 1997. But there was a second part to the prophecy indicating joy would go through the nation just as fast as the mourning did. It is not obvious that this second part has yet been fulfilled, and a book about the prophecy did not attempt to explain the second part of it!

This leads then to the question of how far prophecies today are examined in relation to fulfilment. The New Churches divide prophecies into two broad groups: the 'illuminatory' prophecies, often in picture form, which are taken to encourage the people of God, and are generally not examined in detail for fulfilment, and the 'revelatory' prophecies which often are. There are too many examples today of this latter kind – when political leaders are warned in advance of an assassination attempt, for example – which prove accurate to doubt that prophecy today is for real, and is happening.

Is it *biblical*? That depends on how you define biblical prophecy! Many prophecies today are in pictorial form; clearly that is biblical. Many are given to the church, or the people of God; that too is biblical. Are as many addressed to national leaders as in the Old Testament? Maybe, but not always publicly. Are they tested? Yes, some at least are. Are there major prophets as well as minor prophets? Yes, there are. Is their content negative as well as positive? Apparently so.

Mark Cartledge, then a curate in Formby, Liverpool, wrote an article[32] based on his thesis which looked at the question: Does contemporary prophetic experience correspond to, or cohere with, New Testament prophecy? He looks at the writings of some key theologians, and concludes that there are 'contact points' between the New Testament and today. He cites five areas of agreement:

- Revelatory impulses of some description (words, pictures, dreams, visions) form the basis of prophecy. These impulses are broad in the sense that they contain a variety of experiences.
- The congregational setting is the appropriate and expected context for the exercise of this gift in proclamation.
- Theoretically, anyone can prophesy.
- As a result of prophecy being exercised, the expectations expressed in 1 Corinthians 14:3 should be fulfilled.
- True Christian prophecy is nevertheless a mixed phenomenon and has only an authority of general content, thus requiring discernment and judgement to be exercised by the congregation and its leadership before being accepted.

He concludes that 'contemporary charismatic prophecy is not, by its nature, infallible and in any sense absolute, but rather has a relative authority. Therefore all modern prophecy should be evaluated in light of existing orthodox doctrinal norms, the test of which is Scripture itself.' These seem to me wise words. Undoubtedly some contemporary prophecies have been directly and unambiguously fulfilled, suggesting an authority and a format for expressing that authority. As in all things, the outworkings must be evaluated against the scriptures, in specific not just in general terms.

Prophecy is about change, and is perhaps about creative change. John Adair described the creative perspective leading to a purposeful kind of change[33] as 'the marriage of seen values with the uncreated future ... an extremely dispassionate and realistic gaze: the capacity to see things both as they really are and as they might be'. He then describes the importance of longer-term prophetic utterance, because that is 'about what we are becoming'. The creative person is important to the church because they can help identify new directions.

Sometimes prophecy has been brought into disrepute by false (and forbidden) prophecies of the Second Coming. On the other hand, others enhance prophecy by their fulfilment – like one given to Hudson Taylor, who founded the China Inland Mission in 1865: he paused in the middle of a sermon one day to say he had been given at that moment a prophecy of a coming worldwide war.

Much has been written about prophecy, and whatever our view – and I personally believe it to be very relevant for today – there is no question that very many people especially in New, Pentecostal and other charismatic churches in the UK have heard prophecies, and are expecting God to act. Old and young, men and women, dreaming dreams, seeing visions, and waiting for …

Revival

Revival is much talked about in some circles. In many places, Christians ask God to revive the church, to revive his people, to change this land. Gerald Coates, leader of Pioneer, one of the largest New Church streams, is well known for his frequent expositions of this theme. There is no doubt that we need revival; many of the statistics quoted strongly endorse that. Of course, revival comes from God, and is his sovereign act. But there is no reason why we shouldn't pray for it.

Some would say, Gerald Coates among them, that revival may already be seen if you know where to look. Some ask us to look to North America. The Toronto phenomenon was certainly something different! I visited the Vineyard Church close by Toronto Airport in August 1994, seven months after the slayings in the Spirit began. The preaching was simple and relevant, but was it *revival*? Probably not, but we should not dismiss it, since after five years it still carries on. Tony Higton, the former rather controversial vicar of Hawkwell, Essex, summed up his impressions as 'I have no doubt whatsoever that this was a work of the Holy Spirit'.[34] Others would disagree. But he did not call it *revival*.

What of Pensacola, where some 2.5 million people have attended Brownsville Assembly of God and some 330,000 have responded to the call to repent? Some might well call this a localised revival.[35]

And in the UK? In an article in the *Church of England Newspaper*, Gerald Coates quoted the enormous response to the Alpha courses put on by Holy Trinity Brompton, the huge current interest in Christianity among the police, the resurgence of faith amongst gypsies, and the enormous concern for teaching and information in our prisons – involving perhaps a tenth of all prisoners – as evidence of current revival activity. Revival? These could be the signs, even if localised in different sectors. There has been much prayer for revival in Marsham Street, Westminster, where many people have 'got right with God'. Gerald's summary? 'In large flourishing churches and in a lot of other low profile ways, we are experiencing something extraordinary that has never happened before.'[36] Or at least, not for a very long time.

In October 1998 Alpha courses were being held in 6,300 churches in England and Wales (15% of all churches). R T Kendall, minister of influential Westminster Chapel said, 'It would be a mistake to claim that a great revival has come, but great winds are blowing.'[37] 'Revival,' says Mark Stibbe, vicar of St Andrew's, Chorleywood, 'occurs when the church has become a weak minority, and is God's means of counteracting spiritual decline and creating spiritual momentum.'[38] Conferences are being held on revival, Bible weeks talk of it, and at least one prominent minister has talked about 'days of vision and fulfilment of vision'. Is the expectation really there?

There is another side. Some 30,000 British Christians flew to Toronto in 1997, in search of blessing, an estimated £25 million in airline tickets alone. But total income for the relief and development agency Tearfund that year was just £24 million. Where are our priorities, some would ask, as did the leader of one large evangelical church in the Midlands who wrote to me. Others declare that revival is a 'drug'.[39]

I stand between these lines of argument, and want to be pragmatic. I agree with the conclusions of George Barna when he wrote:[40]

- Pastors are more likely to claim revival than lay people, as it is easy to interpret the high level of spiritual interest currently being shown as evidence of a deeper awakening.
- There are very wide differences in how people define 'revival'. Is it increased church attendance? Evidence of spiritual transformation? Other definitions? If we cannot agree a definition, how do we agree it is happening?
- Research shows that ministers assume that lay people believe the things they themselves believe. The truth is that lay people pick and choose what they want to believe! That's true for revival also.
- Mobilising lay people in revival may be more difficult than expected. Preaching contributes to personal change, but rarely to transformation of life.
- Revival is a popular subject; no one wants to be against it. The number who are passionately, consistently and strategically committed to facilitating it may be fewer than assumed.
- We need to be careful how we talk of revival in our nation. If there is no measurable change in church attendance as a consequence, we simply shoot ourselves in the foot. Revival has to be measurable.

The last point is particularly important. But there is no doubt that the time is ripe for revival! We are indeed a nation with a weak minority of Christians.

Rapture

Some denominations, as the Elim Pentecostal Church used to be, are very clear where they stand on the return of Christ. They took what is called the 'pre-millennial' position. Others take no position at all! Much depends on the interpretation of Matthew 24, the Olivet Discourse, so called because Jesus answered his disciples' question about the future while speaking on the Mount of Olives. He spoke about the forthcoming destruction of the great Temple in Jerusalem, but also gave indications of a far wider catastrophe when he talked of false Christs, wars, famines and tribulations. Was this teaching just relating to the Roman destruction of Jerusalem in AD 70, or did it relate to the end of all things?

There are some certainties on which most agree:

- God will punish the earth for its wickedness
- many feel there will be a 1,000-year reign of Christ
- there are going to be signs and warnings before the end comes
- Christians (the 'saints') will be taken to heaven to be with Christ

Within these very broad parameters, there are various positions, roughly summarised as:[41]

- **Pre-tribulational rapture** Christians are taken to heaven before the punishment of God and before the signs of the end.
- **Mid-tribulational rapture** Christians are taken to heaven before the punishment of God, but after the signs of the end have begun.
- **Post-tribulational rapture** Christians are taken to heaven after the punishment of God.
- **Pre-wrath rapture** This is somewhere between the last two. Christians are taken to heaven before the punishment of God, but after the wrath of Satan has begun. The latter is after the signs of the end and is the period of persecution by Antichrist.

The order of events in Matthew 24 is false Christs, wars, famines and earthquakes – all 'but the beginning of the birth pangs'. Why is this subject important? It is very rarely preached about in the mainline churches, and there is a vast ignorance of end-time things. The Alpha course, which has helped so many to a real and fuller Christian life, makes no mention of the return of Christ.

Some are preaching very vehemently that the end is coming soon. *Earthquake in the City* says, 'the economy of the whole world is unstable and ready for collapse'.[42] That may be true, but the authors make clear that they see such an event as the judgement of God. Others in the United States have written likewise. Others have predicted that Armageddon is coming in 2033,[43] despite clear warnings by Jesus that no one knew the future time of the end, not even he himself! Others say that 'there are just two Popes left before the church is destroyed and the world changed'.[44] Such comments could be multiplied, and have been made almost every decade over the last 2,000 years. As the year 2000 approached, many, perhaps especially in North America, saw doom in every circumstance.[45] The religious writer Damien Thompson's book *The End of Time: Faith and Fear in the Shadow of the Millennium*[46] was published in 1999. So what's new?

Consider this letter which Christian Research received in August 1998, from a named person with address (which, to be fair, we haven't checked out to see if it's genuine). 'I'm writing this letter to you because I have a message from God. He has asked me to tell as many people as I can about his joyous news. The Messiah was born seventeen years ago and he is my youngest son and his name is Drew. I have put my trust in God that you believe what I have told you and hope you will tell all you know the good news as well.' We don't get many letters like that!

Wars? There has never been a century without them, and the twentieth century was the worst of all. In 1990 there were thirty-one major conflicts in the world.[47]

Famines? Ethiopia and Band Aid pictures from the mid-1980s are burnt into memories through the horrific TV pictures we saw then. And since? Somalia, Sudan, North Korea are all countries repeatedly in the news because of their starving and dying peoples.

Earthquakes? In the first twenty-five years of the twentieth century there were six major earthquakes (measuring 7.0 or more on the Richter scale). Between 1925 and 1949 there were another eight of like size; between 1950 and 1975 there were eleven, and between 1975 and 1997 there were twenty-three (and another sixteen between 6.0 and 6.9)!

Other events? In the first fifty years of the twentieth century there were six major volcanic eruptions – in the second fifty years ten; there have been thirteen tsunamis (tidal waves), and ninety-two floods, *half* in the period 1991-97.

What does all this prove? Nothing, but it *could* suggest that the signs of the end of the age are at least beginning. That could be followed by a period of persecution, the wrath of Satan before he faces judgement also. Could persecution come to the UK? At a rather dramatic moment in Spring Harvest 1993, Alex Buchanan, a New Church leader involved with the leadership, asked if he could bring a serious word from God to the evening meeting. He was allowed to do so, and said that he believed that persecution against Christians in the UK would begin by the year 2003. Is there anything to support such? Consider:

- the number of attacks on churches: there were 289 fires in buildings of worship in 1994, 296 in 1996 and 280 in 1997[48]
- the growing level of hatred, often extremely violent and blatant in teenagers and some in their twenties; some will be in positions of leadership in 2003; part of their anger is directed against the church

because it hasn't taken a firm moral stand which might have prevented some of the marriage break-ups in society, the effects of which they have felt personally
- the growing anti-Christian slant in both our culture and laws
- the number who disbelieve in God has tripled in the last fifty years
- the constant media portrayal of violence, and the frustration of young people regarding employment, gives both education on how to wreck society and the motivation for it
- the increasing influence of the occult
- the increasing drift away from the Bible and biblical standards, even among Christians

These will not necessarily lead to persecution, and other factors could help or hinder such action. These include:

- the growing influence of other religions in our country, and an increasing deference to their demands: the start of Islamic schools, for instance, and the willingness of the government to put a question on religion in the 2001 census in England and Wales partly because the Muslims wanted it!
- a growing sense of disillusionment which will probably set in much more deeply once the temporary euphoria of the new Millennium has passed
- we lack quality leadership with moral fibre in political, educational, media, judicial, commercial, industrial and royal life; many key wise, godly leaders have died in recent years, and we do not seem to be replacing them in equal numbers

How is this relevant? How much are we preparing people for persecution? How much do we teach people the importance of staying true to the end? If national revival comes, let us rejoice. It did in Cambodia in 1974 just before the Americans pulled out in 1975 and unleashed Pol Pot and the Killing Fields. Consider the riots in Indonesia and the burning of churches there, the killing of Christians in India and Pakistan. Why should the UK be immune?

Are we less regular at church? What are we preaching? How are women's gifts being used? What are we praying for, and when, and for how long? Do we believe the modern prophets? Do we expect, or teach, revival? Are we anticipating persecution and the rapture? What *are* we doing?

Whither Christianity?

David Edwards, former Provost of Southwark Cathedral and a church historian of no mean repute, wrote in his most recent book, 'Because the decline of the Churches has been so substantial and because their faults and failures have been so hard to deny, it seems likely that for most of the English what survives of Christianity will continue to be more or less churchless unless the churches become radically different.'[1] A churchless Christianity or a peopleless Christianity!

Cyclical movements

Sigmoid curves are essentially mathematical curves which increase initially and then begin to tail off. Charles Handy applies that growth and decline to what happens with products and services. The tailing-off period, inevitable for every product, is the opportunity to create a new product while the sales of the existing are still sufficiently good to cover the costs of creation, production and marketing. This is a well-tried theory which has been shown to work on numerous occasions.

Figure 17: A sigmoid curve, first and second cycles

The theory may, however, also be applied to organisations, including Christian ones. Since the early 1980s there has been a good number of key Christian initiatives in Britain, some very high profile. They have gone through the process of growth and in many cases are beginning to lose market. Take Spring Harvest, for example. It began in the last years of the 1970s, went on to take evangelical church life in Britain by storm in the 1980s, particularly after one of its leaders, Clive Calver, became the General Director of the Evangelical Alliance. It grew rapidly. By 1990 perhaps one in eight of the evangelicals in the UK had been to Spring Harvest. It spread to four different sites in Britain, and at its peak attracted over 80,000 people. It is still very effective, still an important place to go for a holiday-with-a-difference and the opportunity to learn creatively on a vast array of topical issues from a Christian viewpoint. Its evening sessions are tremendously challenging. But it now attracts only 70,000 people, according to the latest brochure, though this is still a huge number. It has tried to renew itself by branching into Europe, but as yet this has not succeeded. It is beginning to come down the sigmoid curve, but a new leadership team announced in 1999 may enable it to climb anew.

The same could be said of March for Jesus – a brilliant innovation to encourage people to pray for the cities especially of the country where they lived. Nearly fifty million people in 177 nations have marched worldwide for Jesus so far.[2] The organisers have announced that the 2000 March will be the last, perhaps because they have been finding it increasingly difficult to maintain momentum in recent years.

The Christian Resources Exhibition began in the mid-1980s and speedily outgrew the Westminster Horticultural Halls. It has been at Sandown Park in Esher, Surrey, since 1987. It has spawned regional exhibitions, both within England and in the other countries in the UK. Its total number of visitors is impressive and much good work is done, but the numbers have stopped growing rapidly, and are perhaps beginning to move along the top of the sigmoid curve.

The same pattern may be observed today in many other important elements of church life, and especially evangelical church life. Graham Kendrick's songs, though still immensely popular, are perhaps sweeping the board less than they once did. The Fellowship of Independent Evangelical Churches grew strongly in the 1970s and 1980s, but is finding it harder to keep numbers up in the 1990s. The Pentecostal churches have been known for radical church planting in many parts of Britain, but there is less enthusiasm (not, note, no enthusiasm) today. The 'Toronto Blessing' was very popular in the mid-1990s but is less so today. Bible Weeks have come and gone, though Stoneleigh still does great things. The Willow Creek Association had some very successful conferences in this country, but today is perhaps less powerful than it was. In 1992, Challenge 2000 forecast 20,000 new churches by the year 2000, but has had to retract that, and is in the process of reformulation at present.

There is no suggestion of criticism in any of these accounts. They are simply stating that the British church experienced a huge amount of experimentation and energy and enthusiasm in the last two decades of the twentieth century. Without doubt, many people have been helped, many encouraged, many who might have fallen away have been kept. There have been many conversions and much spiritual deepening, but, on the simple measure of church attendance, for example, the church, for all this, has not grown.

We are not at the end of experimentation either. Alpha launched a nationwide programme in September 1998. Celtic Christianity is extremely popular, especially the books by David Adam. People continue to attend Taizé in good numbers. The Orthodox Church continues to grow in membership and influence in the UK. But does this all amount to much?

The question is not when will our particular sigmoid curve die, but what is the new curve? We are all having to find how to react and move in the new world of today. Someone said that the search through all these events is like an unborn baby, the church searching for itself. We have had a lot of trial and error, which is good, but little research and development. Where is, has been, the strategic thinking that is required?

Leadership

In a society moving rapidly from one thing to another, with the rate of change increasing, stewards are needed. Can the church be a steward? Leadership needs to be low-key and persuasive. In business terms, we have failed, because we have come round the sigmoid curves without finding the new products. In a firm, that management would be fired! But, it will be argued, the church is not a business. Our calling is to find out what Jesus is doing and join him in doing it. Both parts of this argument are true, because we partly find out what God is about as we launch out into the deep in a new enterprise.

'The leaders of the churches will have to find their own roles in religious communities which share at least something of the general scepticism about leaders,' wrote David Edwards.[3]

What then must be done? George Barna, facing a similar question for American Christianity, has three answers:[4]

- We must motivate people to pursue, embrace and live according to a biblical world-view.
- We must allow the church to be led by the people whom God has called and anointed for that task – that is, leaders.
- We must develop new forums and formats through which people will experience, understand and serve God.

I agree with all these, but wonder if a further component isn't also required – in a word, vision, and behind that, strategy. The second comes out of the first. The other day I was given the strategic plan of a large Christian organisation in America, which had worked out exactly what it was going to do in which countries, God willing, over the next five years. It was a brilliant full-colour, multi-diagrammed, inspirational plan. It was labelled 'building on the vision', but nowhere did it state what the vision was! We must know what it is we aim to become *before* we work out how to get there.

Horizon Mission Methodology

Vision must motivate. To do that it must be built on values. The old way of working out vision is epitomised in my book *Vision Building*, and looks at the reason why your church or organisation exists (your 'purpose') and what you are currently actually doing (your 'mission statement'). In the light of these, a 'vision statement' is worked out, based on questions such as, 'What will you have become in, say, five years' time?', or 'What will be different in the world as a result of your work over the next five years?' There is nothing wrong with the sequence implied here; I have had the privilege of leading scores of churches and organisations in vision-building workshops built around such premises. It is a logical process, full of linear thinking, very acceptable to people of my generation!

In the 1990s, however, a new process came about through the work of the National Aeronautical Space Administration (NASA) in the United States. 'What will the world be like in 2100?' they asked themselves one day. Part of their answer was that by then men would be living on the moon and probably on Mars. The next comment was the breakthrough question: 'What must we do between 2000 and 2010 in order that men may live on the moon in 2100?' It is an excellent question. Although that kind of time-scale is inappropriate for churches and Christian organisations, the concept isn't. 'What must you do in the next two years in order to become what you want to become in seven years' time?' is the valid translation of that concept.

This Horizon Mission Methodology, as it is called, tries to find ways of answering that kind of question. It does it by postulating a future scenario which puts everyone in the organisation on a level playing-field. For example, for one church in Liverpool, I said, 'Suppose it is the year 2050. The asteroid that scientists thought was going to miss the earth didn't, and it landed on the Isle of Man. It is now one month after it landed. The Isle of Man, most of Northern Ireland, the west coast of Scotland and north Wales has gone, though the tip of Snowdon is still above water. Liverpool was badly hit. The earthquake knocked down everything above thirty feet – so the church is badly damaged, and those in blocks of flats are homeless. The floodwater stopped just a mile away. Imagine you are the Church Council. What is your programme for the next six months?'

For an international gathering of leaders we had a different proposition, which is probably in total defiance of science! I postulated that by the year 2030 global warming had had catastrophic effects, and one consequence was that everything green instead grew bright red. So we had bright red grass, bright red bushes, bright red trees, etc. Because our eyes were made to look at green grass, green trees and so on, by the time everyone got to their mid-twenties, they were going blind through the strain. The only people who escaped were those who grew up where there was no vegetation – the nomads in the Saharan Desert or the Inuit in northern Canada. These people effectively became the new world leaders because they could see. As a body of international church leaders, what should the programme be to enable us to continue proclaiming the gospel effectively after 2030?

I am sure you can think of other such way-out examples. The value of them is that they are outside the experience of everyone present. You have to start thinking in new paradigms to cope. It stretches your imagination as a consequence. You have to perceive what it would be like in those circumstances. Having asked each group to report back what they would do, I then ask them, 'Why did you give the answers that you did?' so that their motivations become apparent. In Liverpool we got answers like:

- need to share our resources
- important to set up a communication network
- people are bewildered and need help
- it is an opportunity to share the gospel

The answers were actually in that sort of order. In other words, when the chips were down, this particular group of people tended to react to help people first and preach second. Whether that is the right or wrong order can be debated, but it was their order, and it is therefore on their ordering of their values that you move to the next phase.

This next phase is to postulate a second scenario totally different from the first, to see if the values that were driving them were different or whether the first list should be augmented. I have found that invariably there is an augmentation.

The third phase is then to give a third scenario, much closer in time. An example, again using the Liverpool experience, would be, 'You have a new bishop coming to visit your church next September (year 2005). What are the key items of your programme you wish to show him/her?' This time the aim is to identify the items which will have changed or been improved in the interim period. You then end up with a list of motivations, a list of changes and a list of improvements, and the order in each is then prioritised. Looking at the top two or three in each list, it is readily possible to identify key programme elements required to make up the new vision, and to develop a strategy towards it. In Liverpool, it was to build a new church hall, so that both young and old in that community could have a focal point to meet. The existing church hall, unsuitable for adaptation to such a purpose, would be sold as old people's housing.

This then, in brief, is how I lead vision-building workshops now, using this new Horizon Mission Methodology. It is based on values and creativity. Answers cannot be guessed beforehand. It leads as a consequence to motivation and commitment. In the first decade of the twenty-first century we must be driven by such to establish our vision. And once we have our vision, we can then work out our strategy.

Sound values

Patrick Dixon's book, *Futurewise*,[5] contains so many predictions about the future that it is bewildering! But in the midst of multifaceted change, enduring values will be in increasing demand. 'In a fast, urban, tribal, universal, radical and ethical world of the future, there will be an increasing demand for things which are constant, which never change. When family life is collapsing, relationships are under pressure, jobs appear and disappear, the town you grew up in is unrecognisable and everything else seems to be constantly changing, there is a deep human need to find stability and inner peace.'

How likely is it, then, that the Christian church can keep its values? At present, apart from Northern Ireland, it is *not* unlawful to discriminate against someone on the grounds of religion, though the government is considering changing this. But what is 'religion'? Does it assume certain lifestyles, and could the absence of these constitute a ground for discrimination? Several years ago, the London City Mission were denied their grant by Lewisham Borough Council in Greater London because they refused to allow homosexuals to join their staff, because they felt this lifestyle was inconsistent with their Christian belief.

In 1997 the Church of Scotland indicated that they wished to retain their Christian philosophy in running one of their care homes, which was supported by the local authority. The authority promptly told them their services would no longer be needed and put the patients elsewhere. The home is now closed, and the former staff out of work.

The Roman Catholic Church has a huge stake in the educational system of our country (the Church of England has also, although not on the same scale). In advertisements for teachers, the Catholics ask for those who have been baptised and the Church of England for communicants. This is regarded as discrimination, but is justified on the grounds of it being 'part of the historical agreement'. With the government now fully supporting one Sikh and two Muslim schools, this argument now has current precedent, as obviously Sikhism and Islam are as much discriminating factors as Christianity.

While our judicial system holds, Christian values have a reasonable chance of survival. One of the major concerns of the Old Testament prophets was the abuse of the judicial system within both Israel and Judah. It seems that judges were willing to be bribed and thus abused their position of trust. In the UK today, there does not appear to be any drift towards this kind of corruption. Because we are not perfect, there will always be the occasional miscarriage of justice, which the media avidly pounce on. But the overall numbers of such compared to the total number of cases heard are very small, even if there seems to have been an increase during the 1990s. There is no suggestion that our judges can be systematically bought or individual cases misheard. The widow and the orphan, and others who are disadvantaged, may still get legal redress in the courts of our land. The prophet Zechariah pleads for 'true and sound judge-ment in your courts',[6] and these characteristics still pervade the English judiciary. Perhaps we should applaud it more than we do; many of our judges, including some of the more senior ones, are known as Christians.

However, trying to ensure the maintenance of sound values does not mean that we do not have an absolute moral maze at present. 'Our popular culture is increasingly swept along by privatised and relative values. It is a culture in which Kilroy or Jerry Springer are likely to be moral mentors on a par with the average church leader.'[7] The church will also face increasing difficulties on such matters as abortion and euthanasia; how do we determine acceptable values in such areas?

The Statler Brothers are American country singers. One of their lyrics has a haunting, tragic quality, which reflects the values of our age:[8]

> Tommy's sellin' used cars,
> Nancy's fixin' hair.
> Harvey runs a groc'ry store,
> And Margaret doesn't care.
> Jerry drives a truck for Sears
> And Charlotte's on the make
> And Paul sells life insurance
> And part-time real estate.
>
> And the class of '57 had its dreams.
> We all thought we'd change the world
> With our great works and deeds: Or
> Maybe we just thought the world
> Would change to fit our needs.
> The class of '57 had its dreams.
>
> Betty runs a trailer park,
> Jan sells Tupperware.
> Randy's in an insane ward
> And Mary's on welfare;
> Charley took a job with Ford,
> Joe took Freddy's wife.
> Charlotte took a millionaire
> And Freddy took his life.
>
> But the class of '57 had its dreams
> Ah, the class of '57 had its dreams.

The Millennium

This book was written at the dawn of the third Millennium. What does that even mean? Many believe it's a kind of mechanism which will shape people's future thinking, and their needs and wants in the process. Some fear it, others await it eagerly. Two market researchers identified some of the trends linked to the Millennium.[9] They found that many saw it as being something that promised a positive future – it was not just 'another New Year or Anniversary. The Millennium is an opportunity to walk into a New World'. It was a 'master trend', shaping and directing other trends. They suggested it would yield four possible groups of people, defined by their likely behaviour:

- **the Pathfinders**, who would be drawn to twenty-first-century products to give 'edge', and would therefore abandon old-fashioned products; the 'busters' were most likely to feel this, they said, but the 'boomers' and 'builders' would not be far behind
- **the Followers**, who used products legitimised by the Pathfinders
- **the Conflicted**, who would desire products with some continuity between past and future
- **the Antagonists**, who would hold on to current product choices longer, but, if forced, would seek products that would bridge eras

Supposing they are right, and we substitute 'church' for 'product' in the above sentences. What kind of church would we find? One which was positive, optimistic, refreshingly different, allowing individual reflection but giving clear anchors to life? There is an inner spiritual drive in this 'There's more to me than what you see' – reflecting the personal change many want. Millennium churches will show people how to change, and what discipleship means in practice. Affirmation and encouragement will be key features, with family or other groups very important. Experimentation and entrepreneurship (reflected in part in where people holiday) will be important, and a person's next job will not necessarily follow from his past one. Personal fulfilment will be important, allowing Christ to do his transforming work in people's lives.

The 'mosaics' will, however, think with vigour and freshness, seeking new models and new heroes. Experience and celebration will be key. Are we ready for the challenge they will bring us? Dr George Carey, speaking at a review of the Decade of Evangelism in March 1999, said that mission meant engaging with society: 'If we are to bring people to God, we need a distinctive prophetic witness which engages with our particular culture.'[10] Surely that must include the new millennial culture.

Fall of the Roman Empire

As we look to the future to answer the question 'Whither Christianity?' is there any merit in trying to learn from history, even if in a postmodern world 'all that history teaches us is that history teaches us nothing'? Why did the Roman Empire – that bastion of what was then modernity, in which Christianity was born and grew – tumble out of existence fifteen centuries ago?

Some of the reasons are peculiar to the Roman situation, but not all. One book on the topic identified six key reasons:[11]

- **the failure of the army:** (effectively the police force), because the generals were against the state, and the people were against the army ('quality, spirit and discipline of soldiers not what they were')
- **the gulf between the classes:** the poor were against the state because of massive taxation, the rich were against the state, which allowed them to opt effectively out of leadership, and the middle classes were against the state because inflation had ruined them, and it had been their culture which kept society together
- **the credibility gap:** because the people were against the bureaucrats who came to dominate society, allowing justice to be perverted; the people were against the Emperor, who lived a cloistered life and did not understand common life
- **the partnerships that failed:** when the western and eastern Roman Empires disastrously went their own ways; there was also race against race, because of the many minorities in the population
- **the groups that opted out:** the drop-outs of society who just distanced themselves from the rest of society; the coercion of the state on the grounds of religion; the divisions within Christianity and 'the other world against this world' when many Christians opted out of public life because it was deemed to be 'mammon'
- **the undermining of effort:** complacency was rife: 'new problems will be solved just as the old ones were'; self-help was belittled

The eastern Roman Empire did not fall until 1453, because it was less vulnerable to external attack, had a sounder social and economic structure, was more popular and had a greater internal political stability.

Are any of these reasons relevant today? We do not as yet see Christians opting out of the social life of the country – indeed the reverse seems to be the case. Might they then be blamed if all does not go well? Our political ties exist, though whether they are trusted is a moot point. While there are drop-outs, these have not reached large proportions yet. Taxation is not yet prohibitive. The army is trusted still. Royalty is less distanced than it was as a result of the death of Diana, Princess of Wales.

On the other hand, Christianity is not united. We have many strangers in our midst. We have an increasingly negative and belittling media representation of anything upright and good. The police are less well regarded than they were – and may find getting more recruits increasingly difficult. Negative discrimination against Christianity can be detected, as in the staffing examples already mentioned.

The signs are still largely favourable, suggesting that society itself is unlikely to change radically in the next couple of decades at least. But where will the church be?

Whither Christianity?

Given a society likely to be tolerably stable, but one in which there is increased erosion of biblical foundations and much stronger competition from other religions, what are the changes which the church might see in the first and second decades of the twenty-first century? Here are ten suggestions:

- a continuing and increased nominalism or notionalism: people will continue to opt out of the church, but not out of their own brand of Christianity
- a smaller church, with perhaps only 4% attending church in say 2015, though this percentage might still be large enough to become a critical mass to challenge society;[12] 'attending church' may not necessarily mean Sunday attendance, as churches switch to more midweek worship services
- smaller churches as individual units, partly because of more church plants, but also because of smaller numbers involved; the cell church will encourage this drift also; female leadership accepted, but some men in some congregations find this unbearable and leave, though in an increasingly matriarchical society, this number may be smaller than some would think
- denominations increasingly less meaningful, and churchmanship becoming less important; church membership therefore becomes less meaningful, and a useless statistic; ultimately this has to threaten the establishment of the Church of England, as will the increasing government demands to spend scarce cash on buildings rather than programme
- fewer clergy, but more lay leadership; full-time clergy will however be more IT-sophisticated, and e-mail linkage will be mandatory, web-sites common
- the cyber-church will be a reality with many using a flat-screen TV on their wall to join a congregation singing a hymn they like in Sydney, Singapore or Seattle; this simply adds to the issue of nominality and the small numbers committed to face-to-face meetings
- the likelihood of an evangelical split, essentially between the charismatics and non-charismatics, though it will be on the issues of prophetic fulfilment on the one hand and the reformed groups on the other, and between the older people adhering to a more classical evangelicalism and younger people whose biblical evangelical basis is much less; possible collapse of the Evangelical Alliance if this really happens
- youth work still of major importance, with a majority of people, say 60%, still finding faith before the age of twenty; a steady stream however of older people coming to faith, or returning to faith.
- difficulty of coping with an increased antagonism to Christianity; torching of churches; much angry, bitter and hateful graffiti

- the Church of England crucial in terms of leadership; voice to the nation; authority of the Archbishop's Council; more resources than any other denomination, even Roman Catholics; hence Anglican priorities become crucial

This list suggests that the late Cardinal Hume's call for a changed society[13] will go largely unheeded. He said that if Britain is to change, we need to be a society that:

- protects and promotes marriage and the family
- ceases to be so obsessed with sex
- ends abortion
- combats racism
- bans irresponsible arms sales
- tackles poverty at home and abroad
- respects the environment as God's gift for our use
- is led by men and women of integrity, worthy of respect
- sees the media rediscovering its responsibility for shaping society's values
- looks beyond the here and now to rediscover spiritual values

Strategic thinking

The new Archbishop's Council 'will enable the Church to tackle strategic issues which need gripping if our mission is to be effective'.[14] Where else is strategic thinking taking place? Who is doing it? *You* can do it! You can do it for your church or your organisation. To start down the track, answer the eight questions listed in the Introduction to this book. There are many texts on the subject, but those questions are an easy way to start.

The 21st century church

What kind of Christian heritage will be left if we run forward to 2040? The Christian scene then is likely to be radically different!

- Far fewer church buildings (30,000+) in the UK, and some of the 5,000 rural Norman churches will still be open.
- Spirituality will not be dead (the religious community will still be 40% of the population and mostly older people), but its Christian proportion will be smaller, as the non-Christian religions will by then have a very significant share (at least a third of this 40%). Implicit religion will flourish.
- The basic doctrines of Christianity will be believed much less, and there will be many who actively do not believe them, even though

they call themselves Christian. Tensions between believers and non-believers could become acute.

- Church attendance will probably be at an all-time low, possibly as low as 0.5% of the population. Church membership likewise will be very small, as society continues to move away from commitment of any kind. New traditions will replace old traditions, with flexibility and time, not money, being the new key values.[15]
- Congregations will be much smaller than they are now, but the charismatic churches will continue to start new ones. Urban congregations will struggle more than rural ones.
- Christianity will continue to exert some influence on the life of the nation, though baptism and marriage in church will be much less popular. Funerals, however, will continue to be opportunities for spiritual reality.
- There will still be many Christian organisations (2,000+), but probably far fewer, if any, Christian bookshops as literature (including religious material) will be available through electronic means.
- A booming cyberchurch, widespread use of electronic means of communication, and worship conducted in myriad ways over the Internet.
- Midweek worship services rather than on Sunday mornings especially in the non-institutional churches. Flexibility will be the key characteristic.

Unless, of course, there is revival or the Lord Jesus Christ returns!

In summary, then: a small Christian core valuing integrity,[16] a continuing wider, vaguer, Christian penumbra, with a religious fringe beyond that including other religions. Belief will be real for the few, but disappearing in the many. But despite all the differences, and the trends which we would regard as inimical to Christianity, it will still be a world where faith is relevant!

Let the final word go to Billy Graham, who at the Berlin Congress on Evangelism in 1966 said:[17]

> 'One of the purposes of this World Congress on Evangelism is to make an urgent appeal to the world church to return to the dynamic zeal for world evangelisation that characterised Edinburgh fifty-six years ago. The evangelistic harvest is always urgent. Every generation is crucial; every generation is strategic. But we are not responsible for the past generation, and we cannot bear full responsibility for the next one. However, we do have our generation! God will hold us responsible at the Judgement Seat of Christ for how well we fulfilled our responsibilities and took advantage of our opportunities.'

Notes

The European Context

1 Rev Dr David Barrett, 'Status of Global Mission', in *International Bulletin of Missionary Research*, Connecticut, January 1998, p27.

2 Professor A H Halsey, in collaboration with Jo Webb, *British Social Trends 1900-2000*, Macmillan, London, 1999, Ch.1.

3 Mark 4:18.

4 Mark 4:19.

5 Paper by Rev Dr Eddie Gibbs, Professor of Church Growth at Fuller Theological Seminary, Los Angeles, Ca., USA.

6 Heather Wraight (ed.), *They Call Themselves Christian*, Christian Research and Lausanne Committee, London and Carlisle, 1999.

7 Professor David Martin, *Tongues of Fire*, Blackwell, Oxford, 1990.

8 In the 1989 English Church Census, some denominations had an attendance larger than membership: Baptists (85 average attendance to membership of 73), Independents, including the New Churches (71 to 51) and Pentecostals (95 to 72).

9 Initial results from a sample of churches undertaking the Congregational Attitudes and Beliefs Survey in 1998.

10 Information Service of the German Evangelical Alliance, English Edition, November 1998.

11 Professor William L Wagner, North American Missionaries in Europe, Doctor of Theology Thesis, University of South Africa, 1989.

12 The apt sub-title to Dr Grace Davie's book, *Religion in Britain since 1945*, Blackwell, Oxford, 1994.

Church People in the UK

1 *Guardian* report by Sarah Hall, 24 August 1998.

2 *Daily Telegraph* report by Victoria Coombe, 14 December 1998.

3 *Time Magazine* report by Charles Krauthammer, 15 June 1998.

4 Mary Lawson (ed.), *Austrian Christian Handbook*, MARC Europe, London, 1991, p15.

5   Dr Peter Brierley (ed.), *World Churches Handbook,* Christian Research and Lausanne Committee for World Evangelization, London, 1997, p10.

6   Dr Peter Brierley (ed.), *Irish Christian Handbook 1995/96,* Christian Research, London, 1994, p21.

7   For example, Patrick Johnstone in *Operation World,* OM Publishing, Carlisle, 1993.

8   Dr Peter Brierley (ed.), *Religious Trends No. 1 1998/99,* Christian Research and Paternoster Publishing, London and Carlisle, 1997.

9   Dr Peter Brierley (ed.), *World Churches Handbook,* Christian Research and Lausanne Committee for World Evangelization, London, 1997.

10 Report in *Church of England Newspaper,* 23 August 1996.

11 See, for example, Robert Currie, Alan Gilbert and Lee Horsley, *Churches and Churchgoers,* Oxford University Press, Oxford, 1977.

12 David Longley and Peter Brierley (eds), *UK Christian Handbook 1987/88,* MARC Europe, London, 1986, Table 9a, p135, Footnote 2.

13 Dr Kent R Hunter, 'Ask the Church Doctor', in *Strategies for Today's Leader,* Vol. XXXIII, No.2, Fall 1996, p13.

14 *Scotreach Programme Report,* Baptist Union of Scotland, 1988, p7.

15 Heather Wraight and Dr Peter Brierley (eds), *UK Christian Handbook 1996/97,* Christian Research, London, 1995, Table 9a, p240.

16 Reported in Peter Brierley, *'Christian' England,* and *Prospects for the Nineties,* both MARC Europe, London, 1991.

17 Rev Fergus Macdonald and Peter Brierley, *Prospects for Scotland 2000,* National Bible Society of Scotland, Edinburgh, and Christian Research, London, 1995.

18 Peter Kaldor, and others, *Winds of Change,* The National Church Life Survey, Lancer, NSW, Australia, 1994, p263.

19 George Barna, *Casting the Net,* 'The Unchurched Population', Barna Research Group, LA, California, USA, 1995, p3.

20 European Values Systems Study 1990, quoting Dr Peter Brierley (ed.), *Religious Trends No.1 1998/99,* Christian Research and Paternoster Publishing, London and Carlisle, Table 2.5.2.

21 The results are published annually in separate volumes, but there was also the *British Social Attitudes Cumulative Source Book,* covering 1983–89.

22 Dr Peter Brierley (ed.), *Religious Trends No. 1 1998/99,* Christian Research and Paternoster Publishing, London and Carlisle, 1997, Table 2.12.4.

23 As above, Table 2.2.

24 *Third Way* article by David Lyon, July 1984.

25 See for example 'Introduction' by Dr Grace Davie to *Religious Trends*

No.1 1998/99, Christian Research and Paternoster Publishing, London and Carlisle, 1997, p0.3.

26 *World Prayer News*, Sept/Oct 1998, Evangelical Missionary Alliance, London, Day 2.

27 1998 English Attendance Survey results as quoted in *The Tide is Running Out*, Peter Brierley, Christian Research, London, 2000.

28 Preb Rodney Schofield, 'Newcomers hidden behind the numbers', *Church Times*, 7 February 1997.

29 *British Social Attitudes Cumulative Source Book*, Gower and Social and Community Planning Research, Dartmouth and London, 1992.

30 Taken from figures given by Dr Grace Davie at the Sociology of Religion Study Group meeting of the British Sociological Association in April 1997, which in turn were adapted from Ashford and Timms' book of 1992.

31 Peter Kaldor, and others, *Winds of Change*, The National Church Life Survey, Lancer, NSW, Australia, 1994, p344.

32 As above, p106.

33 Dr Peter Brierley, *The Tide is Running Out*, Christian Research, London, 2000.

34 Reported in *The Times*, 27 November 1996.

35) As above.

36 European Values Study, as quoted by *Religious Trends No.1 1998/99*, Christian Research and Paternoster Publishing, 1997, Table 2.5.2.

37 Professor Marcus J. Borg, *The God We Never Knew*, Harper, San Francisco, USA, 1997.

38 Matthew 7:22; 25:12.

39 Paper by Professor Eddie Gibbs in Heather Wraight (ed.), *They Call Themselves Christian*, Christian Research and Lausanne Committee, London and Carlisle, 1999.

40 Lesley Walmsley, compiler, *C S Lewis on Faith*, HarperCollins, London, 1998, p13.

41 Mission & Evangelism Resources Committee, 1995, *Understanding the Times*, Church of Scotland, St Andrew Press, Edinburgh, 1995, p36.

42 Rev Chris Sugden (ed.), *Death of a Princess*, Silver Fish Publishing, London, 1998, p18.

43 As above, p20.

44 George Barna, *Casting the Net*, 'The Unchurched Population', Barna Research Group, LA, California, USA, 1995, pp6,7.

45 Rev Chris Sugden (ed.), *Death of a Princess*, Silver Fish Publishing, London, 1998, p40.

46 Article by Professor Andrew Greeley, Professor of Social Science at Chicago University, from a summary in the *Church Growth Digest*,

Vol.14, No.2, 1997, p6, based on *British Social Attitudes Survey 1997*, Social and Community Planning Research, 14th Report, London.

47 Rev Chris Sugden (ed.), *Death of a Princess*, Silver Fish Publishing, London, 1998, p32.

48 Professor A H Halsey, in collaboration with Jo Webb, *British Social Trends 1900-2000*, Macmillan, London, 1999, Ch.1.

49 Rev Chris Sugden (ed.), *Death of a Princess*, Silver Fish Publishing, London, 1998, p33.

50 Report in the *Daily Telegraph*, 5 February 1997.

51 Dr Patrick Dixon, *Futurewise*, HarperCollins, London, 1998.

52 Review in *Church of England Newspaper*, 30 October 1998, p7.

Church Ministers in the UK

1 Numbers for other professions taken from *Lifestyle Pocket Book*, Advertising Association with NTC Publications, Henley-on-Thames, Oxon, 1993, p33.

2 Dr Peter Brierley (ed.), *Religious Trends No. 1, 1998/99*, Christian Research and Paternoster Publishing, London and Carlisle, 1997, Sections 2, 8 and 9.

3 Private survey by Christian Research, December 1998.

4 Professor A H Halsey (ed.), *British Social Trends since 1900*, Macmillan, London, 1988, Table 13.17.

5 Dr Peter Brierley (ed.), *Religious Trends No. 2, 2000/2001*, Christian Research, London 1999, Table 5.2.4.

6 See *More Than One Church* Survey Report, MARC Monograph No.26, MARC Europe, London, 1989.

7 Rev Dr Paul Beasley-Murray and Alan Wilkinson, *Turning the Tide*, Bible Society, London, 1981, Fig.9, p33.

8 Rev Robert Schuller, *Your Church has a Fantastic Future!*, Regal, Ca., USA, 1986, p268.

9 Rev Dr Paul Beasley-Murray and Alan Wilkinson, *Turning the Tide*, Bible Society, London, 1981, Fig.9, p33.

10 Proverbs 29:18.

11 *Next* magazine, California, May 1997, p2.

12 As above.

13 'Seven Steps to Restoring your Church', by Stephen L. Bishop, Senior Pastor, Union Church of Bogota, Colombia (Seventh-Day Adventist), in *Ministry*, USA, January 1999, pp 8,9.

14 Rev Robert Schuller, *Your Church has a Fantastic Future!*, Regal, Ca., USA, 1986, p5.

15 *Context*, Spring/Summer 1998, p6.

16 Peter Brierley, *Priorities, Planning and Paperwork*, Monarch, Crowborough, East Sussex, 1992, p45.

17 *Social Trends No.29*, Office for National Statistics, London, 1999.

18 'Christians in Public Leadership', *The Church and the World of Work*, Birmingham, 1993.

19 See successive issues of the *Church of England Year Book*, Church House Publishing, London. In 1988, for example, there were 431 candidates (252 men and 80 women for the stipendiary ministry, and 50 men and 51 women for the non-stipendiary ministry). In 1992 the total was 435, but in 1993 it dropped to 358.

20 Very Rev David Edwards, *A Concise History of Christianity*, HarperCollins Religious, London, 1998, p171.

21 *Church Times* report, 23 October 1998, p2.

22 Report in *Quadrant*, Christian Research, London, November 1998, p1, quoting from research by Mark Greene, Vice-Principal London Bible College, and published in detail in *Anvil*, Vol.14, No.4, 1997.

23 *Third Way* article, 1998, reproduced in *Quadrant*, Christian Research, London, January 1999, p6.

24 *The Bulletin* article, National Council for Christian Standards, Horam, East Sussex, Vol.3, No.2, penultimate page.

25 *Church of England Newspaper* report, 8 October 1998, p2.

26 Reported in the *Express*, 2 November 1998, p15.

27 Rev Robin Gamble, *The Irrelevant Church*, Monarch, Crowborough, East Sussex, 1991.

28 'Towards 2000', in *Together*, Autumn 1998, CPAS, Warwick, p5.

29 *Church Times* report, 9 October 1998, p3.

30 Insight Review in *Christianity*, June 1998, p37.

31 Reported in the *Express*, 2 November 1998, p15.

32 *1998 English Church Attendance Survey* results as quoted in *The Tide is Running Out*, Peter Brierley, Christian Research, 2000.

33 Very Rev David Edwards, *A Concise History of Christianity*, HarperCollins Religious, London, 1998, p171.

34 R Meredith Belbin, *Management Teams*, Butterworth-Heinemann, London, 1981, but reprinted virtually every year since.

35 Undertaken by Rev Canon Rod Anderson, reported in *Quadrant*, Christian Research, London, January 1996, p6.

36 George Barna, *The Second Coming of the Church*, Word Publishing, London, 1998, p36.

37 Rt Rev Gavin Reid, Bishop of Maidstone, 15 October 1998, St Paul's, Onslow Square.

38 Richard Higginson, *Transforming Leadership*, SPCK, London, 1996, p23.

39 'Where are leaders when you need them?' by Alice Thomson, *Daily Telegraph*, 16 September 1998, p20.

40 Richard Higginson, *Transforming Leadership*, SPCK, London, 1996, p26.

41 As above, p61.

42 *Netfax*, Leadership Network, USA, No.100, 22 June 1998, p1.

43 Billy Graham, *Just As I Am*, HarperCollins, London, 1997.

44 As above.

45 Private communication, but a set of the forms is doubtless available from him.

46 'Bosses stay switched on in the sun', in *Management Tomorrow*, Institute of Management's newsletter for student members, Issue 4, 1998/9, p10.

Church and Young People

1 'The Davidson interview: Terry Green', by Andrew Davidson, in *Management Today*, Corby, January 1999, p40.

2 'The Truth is Out There!' by Rev Dr Rowland Croucher, in *Ministry Today*, Issue 14, October 1998, p27.

3 Summary of dissertation 'Mission to the New Young of Japan', sent by e-mail 26 November 1998, and available from INTERNET:kandesan@aol.com.

4 For example, Kevin Ford's *Jesus for a New Generation*, or George Barna's *Generationext*, Regal, Ca., USA, 1995.

5 *Daily Telegraph* report, 24 August 1998, based on study of 500 American families in Iowa, conducted by Dr Valarie King, Penn State University.

6 *Guardian* report, 5 May 1998, on a Family Policy Studies Centre survey, mentioned in the *R Briefing*, Issue 20, August 1998.

7 Based on George Barna, *The Second Coming of the Church*, Word, London, 1998, p72.

8 Dr William Taylor (ed.), *Too Valuable to Lose*, William Carey Library, Pasadena, Ca., USA, 1997, p48.

9 Peter Brierley, *A Century of British Christianity*, MARC Monograph No.14, MARC Europe, London, 1989, p37.

10 See the *Admission to Communion in Relation to Baptism and Confirmation Report*, Church House, 1998, and the previous report of the initial experimentation.

11 See, for example, Rev Andrew Daunton-Fear's letter in *Church Times*, 6 November 1998, p9.

12 Peter Brierley, *Reaching and Keeping Teenagers*, Monarch, Crowborough, East Sussex, 1993, p180.

13 Professor D Martin, *A Sociology of English Religion*, SPCK, New York, 1967, p42.

14 '86% don't hear', by Dave Roberts, in *Renewal*, February 1999, p30.

15 Thomas W Laquer, *Religion and Respectability: Sunday Schools and Working Class Culture 1780-1850*, Yale University Press, USA, 1976. See also Dr Peter Brierley (ed.), *Religious Trends No. 2, 2000/2001*, HarperCollins and Christian Research, London, 1999.

16 George Barna, *The Second Coming of the Church*, Word, London, 1998, p3.

17 'Is there life after Sunday School?' by Martin Lambourne, in *European Christian Bookstore Journal*, March 1998, p31.

18 Rev David Hunt, *Reflecting on our Past, A statistical look at Baptists in Scotland 1892-1997*, November 1997, p15.

19 '86% don't hear', by Dave Roberts, in *Renewal*, February 1999, p30.

20 Chapter 'The Age of Information' by Alan Rogers, in David Porter (ed.), *The Word on the Box*, Paternoster Publishing, Carlisle, p84.

21 Personal letter from Colin and Margaret Booker, December 1998.

22 Peter Brierley, *Reaching and Keeping Teenagers*, Monarch, Crowborough, East Sussex, 1993, Table 49, p182.

23 Rev Chris Sugden (ed.), *Death of a Princess*, Silver Fish Publishing, London, 1998, pp36,47.

24 Comment by a perceptive American missionary working in the UK, January 1999.

25 Rev Alister McGrath and Rev Michael Green, *Springboard for Faith*, Hodder & Stoughton, London, 1994, p53, and quoted in *Understanding the Times*, Church of Scotland, St Andrew Press, 1995, p34.

26 Philip Richter and Professor Leslie Francis, *Gone but not Forgotten*, Darton, Longman and Todd, London, 1998, p137.

27 A summary of this may be found in Peter Brierley, *Reaching and Keeping Teenagers*, Monarch, Crowborough, East Sussex, 1993, pp158-160.

28 Dr Jeff Astley, *How Faith Grows*, Faith Development and Christian Education, National Society/Church House Publishing, London, 1992.

29 Professor Eddie Gibbs, *Winning Them Back*, Monarch, Crowborough, East Sussex, 1993, Table 9, p278.

30 George Barna, *The Second Coming of the Church*, Word, London, 1998, p55.

31 MORI poll of 462 parents, in *Reader's Digest*, October 1994.

32 George Barna, *The Second Coming of the Church*, Word, London, 1998, p58.

33 Private research for a youth organisation by Christian Research, London, December 1998.

34 Rev David Hunt, *What's Going on the Churches?*, A Survey of Baptisms in Scottish Baptist Churches, December 1997, p26.

35 *Baptists Today* report, by Rev Clive Jacobs, in the magazine of the Baptist Union of South Africa, August-October 1998, p5.

36 Extract from a personal letter quoting Robert Warren, August 1998.

37 Dr Peter Brierley, *The Tide is Running Out*, HarperCollins and Christian Research, London, 2000.

38 *Background to the Task*, Scripture Union, 1968; this Report of the 'Commission on Mission' survey for the Evangelical Alliance asked 4,000 people about their conversion.

39 *Finding Faith in 1994*, Survey for Churches Together in England Lent '94 Course, by Christian Research, London, and published in summary in *Quadrant*, March 1998.

40 Dr William K Kay and Professor Leslie J Francis, *Drift from the Churches*, University of Wales Press, Cardiff, 1996.

41 From a Eurobarometer survey report, *Young people on the threshold of the year 2000*, European Commission, Luxembourg, September 1997, p3.

Society and Young People

1 *Social Trends Quarterly*, Pilot Issue, Winter 1998, p5.

2 *Right from Wrong*, a survey of 677 young people attending church in 1997, undertaken by Christian Research for Agapé, published in a special issue of *Quadrant*, Autumn 1997.

3 *Daily Telegraph* report, 24 February 1997, based on 300 interviews of young people aged 16-30.

4 *Daily Telegraph* report, 18 June 1997, based on 3,000 A-level students (mostly studying philosophy or religion) at sixth-form RE conferences in 1996 and 1997, p3.

5 From a Eurobarometer survey report, *Young people on the threshold of the year 2000*, European Commission, Luxembourg, September 1997, p6.

6 Social Trends *Quarterly*, Pilot Issue, Winter 1998, p5.

7 *Knowledge and experience of drug use amongst church-affiliated young people*, by Christopher Cook, Deborah Goddard and Rachel Westall, Evangelical Alliance, London, 1997.

8 Denominational and Sectarian Influence on Adolescent Attitudes toward Drug Use in England and Wales, by Leslie Francis and Kenneth Mullen, *Journal of Alcohol and Drug Education*, Vol.42, No.3, Spring 1997, pp81-96.

9 As above.

10 *Ansvar Survey of English Social Behaviour*, report by Christian Research, London, 1995, with some results published in Dr Peter Brierley (ed.), *Religious Trends No 1 1998/99*, Christian Research and Paternoster Publishing, London and Carlisle, 1997, Table 5.6.2.

11 Mark Twain, *Notebook*, 1935.

12 It may be wondered why the percentages aren't equal since one man is married to one woman! The percentages are of the total population, and as there are more women in the population than men because they live longer, the denominator for the women is larger and the percentage therefore smaller.

13 *Daily Telegraph* report, 9 January 1999, p5.

14 Dr Peter Brierley (ed.), *Religious Trends No 1 1998/99*, Christian Research and Paternoster Publishing, London and Carlisle, 1997, Table 4.9.

15 From a Eurobarometer survey report, *Young people on the threshold of the year 2000*, European Commission, Luxembourg, September 1997, p6.

16 'What about the Children?' by Dr Clifford Hill, in *Prophecy Today*, Vol.14, No.3, May/June 1998, p13.

17 Review *Marriage and its Modern Crisis*, by Alan Storkey, Hodder & Stoughton, London, 1996, in *Anvil*, Vol.14, No.4, 1997, p331.

18 'Children's perspectives on families', Joseph Rowntree Research Report, in *Findings*, July 1998, p1.

19 'Exploding the marriage myth', in *Care Magazine*, Winter 1998/99, p5.

20 Peter Brierley (ed.), *Irish Christian Handbook 1995/96*, Christian Research, London, 1994, Table 4, p24.

21 'What about the Children?' by Dr Clifford Hill, in *Prophecy Today*, Vol.14, No.3, May/June 1998, p12.

22 Based on data in *Social Trends Quarterly*, Pilot Issue, Winter 1998, p4.

23 From a Eurobarometer survey report, *Young people on the threshold of the year 2000*, European Commission, Luxembourg, September 1997, p6.

24 There are some who disagree that giving identical addresses is an

indicator of cohabitation. Some vicars say that couples do this to save fees because they come from different boroughs, or because they don't know where they'll be living and give their in-laws' address instead. While such reasons are undoubtedly true for some, the huge numbers that the government figures indicate show clearly that cohabitation is a popular option, and that this is true for Christian people as well.

25 'Spouses with identical addresses before marriage: an indicator of pre-marital cohabitation', by John Haskey, *Population Trends*, Office for National Statistics, London, Autumn 1997, No.89, p13.

26 'Family Matters', by Dr Clifford Hill, in *Prophecy Today*, Vol.14, No.4, July/August 1998, p10 .

27 As above, p11.

28 Matthew 24:13.

29 Kathleen E Kiernan and Valerie Estaugh, *Cohabitation*, Extra-marital childbearing and social policy, Family Policy Studies Centre, London, 1993, Occasional Paper No.17, p7.

30 Circulated letter from Dr Michael Schluter, The Relationships Foundation, Cambridge, July 1998.

31 Council Meeting of the Evangelical Missionary Alliance, 26 January 1999.

32 Rev Andy Hickford, *Essential Youth*, Kingsway, Eastbourne, 1998, p125.

33 *Social Trends Quarterly*, Pilot Issue, Winter 1998, p7.

34 'What about the Children?' by Dr Clifford Hill, in *Prophecy Today*, Vol.14, No.3, May/June 1998, p11.

35 As above.

36 Based on 'Population Review (9): Summary of issues', by John Craig, in *Population Trends*, Office for National Statistics, London, Summer 1997, No.88, p7.

37 Additional demographic comments are taken from the above article.

38 Dr Patrick Dixon, *Futurewise*, HarperCollins, London, 1998, p94.

39 Miriam E.David (ed.), 'The Fragmenting Family: Does It Matter?', article by John Haskey, Institute of Economic Affairs, Choice in Welfare Series No.44, June 1998, p29.

40 As above, p31.

41 Luke 21:8.

Key Factors of Church Life

1 Dr Peter Brierley (ed.), *Religious Trends No. 2, 2000/2001*, HarperCollins and Christian Research, London 1999.

2 'Convert' may be too strong a description for some of the people included here. Undoubtedly some, probably the majority, will have had a definite experience of conversion, but others have simply started attending church which a year before they did not do. They were outsiders who have become insiders, whether or not they have had a conversion experience.

3 Dr Peter Brierley, Leaders' Briefing No.3, *Changing Churches*, Christian Research, London, 1996.

4 As above; also Professor Eddie Gibbs, *Winning Them Back*, Monarch, Crowborough, East Sussex, 1993.

5 Rev Michael Fanstone, *The Sheep that Got Away*, Monarch, Crowborough, East Sussex, 1993.

6 Professor Eddie Gibbs, *Winning Them Back*, Monarch, Crowborough, East Sussex, 1993.

7 Rev Dr G Wakefield, *Finding a Church: reasons people give for joining and moving from churches*, PhD Thesis, University of Kent at Canterbury, March 1998.

8 Philip Richter and Professor Leslie J Francis, *Gone but not Forgotten*, Darton, Longman and Todd, London, 1998.

9 'Why people don't go to church?' in *Pointers*, Bulletin of the Christian Research Association, Australia, Vol.5, No.3, September 1995, p12.

10 The 1993 survey was undertaken by Mike Ewan, Youth Secretary, Baptist Union of Ireland, and reported in *Quadrant*, Christian Research, London, November 1994, p1.

11 Peter Brierley, *Reaching and Keeping Teenagers*, Monarch, Crowborough, East Sussex, 1993, p148, and the survey behind the book.

12 'One in two preachers aren't relevant', by Mark Greene in *Quadrant*, Christian Research, London, November 1998, p1; also published in more detail in *Anvil*, Vol.14, No.4, 1997.

13 But not always smoothly. See, for example, research by Rev Patsy Kettle, *Ministry and Marriage*, Survey of Women Priests in the Church of England, Leaders' Briefing No.9, Christian Research, London, 1997.

14 Survey undertaken by Christian Research in 1998 sponsored by several women's organisations and women's departments of denominations. Report being written by Heather Wraight for publication in 2000.

15 Congregational Attitudes and Beliefs Survey carried out for churches in Kent and Surrey, 1998

16 Professor C Peter Wagner, *Prayer Shield*, Monarch, Crowborough, East Sussex, 1992, p70.

17 'Does prayer make a difference in church growth?' by Marlin Mull, in *Church Growth Today*, Vol.8, No.5, 1993.

18 *Lifestyle Survey*, Board of Social Responsibility, Church of Scotland, Edinburgh, 1987, p18.

19 Peter Brierley (ed.), *Act on the Facts*, MARC Europe, London, 1992, p177.

20 Dr William Kay and Professor Leslie J Francis, *Drift from the Churches*, University of Wales Press, Cardiff, 1996.

21 Reported in a special issue of *Quadrant*, Autumn 1997, p4.

22 'The effects of prayer on mental well-being', by Margaret Poloma, in *Second Opinion*, Vol.18, No.3, January 1993.

23 Undertaken by *Newsweek* magazine, 31 March 1997, and published in *Leadership*, Winter 1998, p77.

24 Details are available directly from Teal Trust, 11 Lincoln Road, Cramlington, NE23 9XT. Figures given here are extracted from 'The Priorities of Prayer', by the Trust Director, John Preston, in *Quadrant*, Christian Research, May 1999, p1.

25 Dr Billy Graham, *Just as I Am*, HarperCollins, London, 1997, p235.

26 *Prayer Watch*, Morris Cerullo's regular bulletin, Vol.2, November 1998, p1.

27 Newsletter of Roger Carswell, end 1998, p4.

28 'Children playing new role in charismatic churches', in *Religion Watch*, Vol.13, No.11, October 1998, p2.

29 John Adair, *The Becoming Church*, SPCK, London, 1997, p26.

30 Ephesians 4:11.

31 Christopher Hill, *Flowers in the Cities*, Marshall Pickering, 1998, p13.

32 'Charismatic prophecy and New Testament prophecy', by Rev Dr Mark J Cartledge, *Themelios*, October/November 1991, Vol.17, No.1, pp17-19.

33 John Adair, *The Becoming Church*, SPCK, London, 1997, p25.

34 Paper by Rev Tony Higton, *What I really believe about the Toronto Blessing*, Hawkwell, Essex, March 1999, p2.

35 'A small cloud, the size of a hand', by Gerald Coates, in *Renewal*, December 1998, p58.

36 'Evidence of Revival in Britain', interview by Andrew Carey, *Church of England Newspaper*, 15 May 1998, p10.

37 *Church of England Newspaper*, 9 October 1998, p1.

38 Rev Dr Mark Stibbe, *Revival*, Monarch, Crowborough, East Sussex, 1998.

39 *Ship of Fools* Newsletter, 1998, p1.

40 'Spiritual Revival: Is it here or not?' by George Barna, *The Barna Report*, Barna Research Group, Ventura, Ca., USA, January-March 1999, p1.

41 Robert Van Kampen, *The Rapture Question Answered*, Fleming Revell, Michigan, USA, 1997, p39.

42 Clifford Denton and Paul Slennett, *Earthquake in the City*, Kingsway, Eastbourne, 1997.

43 John Denton, *Armageddon AD 2033*, BRIC, London, 1995.

44 John Hogue, *Last Pope*, Element, London, 1998.

45 Article in *Time* magazine, 18 January 1999, pp42-53.

46 Published by Vintage, London, January 1999.

47 These and subsequent figures are taken from appropriate pages in *The Hutchinson Almanac 1999*, Helicon, Oxford, 1998.

48 Home Office Fire Statistics, published also in Dr Peter Brierley (ed.), *Religious Trends, No 1, 1998/99*, Christian Research and Paternoster Publishing, London and Carlisle, 1997, Table 5.5.2; also personal correspondence with the Home Office.

Whither Christianity?

1 Very Rev David L Edwards, *A Concise History of English Christianity*, Fount, HarperCollins, 1998, p166.

2 'Falling in for the Final UK March', in *Celebrate*, Crowborough, East Sussex, March 1999, p21.

3 Very Rev David L Edwards, *A Concise History of English Christianity*, Fount, HarperCollins, 1998, p171.

4 George Barna, *The Second Coming of the Church*, Word, London, 1998, p133.

5 Dr Patrick Dixon, *Futurewise*, HarperCollins, London, 1998.

6 Zechariah 8:16.

7 Minutes of a discussion at the Evangelical Alliance UK Council of Management on 16-17 September, 1998, p3.

8 Taken from Tony Campolo, *Stand Up and be Counted*, Marshall Pickering, HarperCollins Religious, London, 1993, p146. Used by permission.

9 'Projecting the future', by Gene Shore and Peter Cooper, *Journal of the Market Research Society*, Vol.41, No.1, January 1999, pp33-45.

10 *Church of England Newspaper* report by Sarah Meyrick, 12 March 1999.

11 Professor Michael Grant, *The Fall of the Roman Empire*, Annenberg School Press, Nelson and Sons Ltd, London, 1976.

12 The Evangelical Alliance suggests the figure could be three million adults in the UK in 2010, which is 6% (see 7, above).

13 'At the Millennium, let us pray', by Cardinal Basil Hume, *Daily Telegraph*, 17 February 1999.

14 *Church of England Newspaper* article by Andrew Carey, 22 January 1999, p1.

15 George Barna, *The Frog in the Kettle*, Regal, Ventura, Ca., USA, 1990.

16 As above.

17 Dr Billy Graham, *Just As I Am*, HarperCollins, London, 1997, p565.

Index